Fotheringham's Sporting Trivia

The Greatest Sporting Trivia Book Ever...

Printed and bound in Great Britain by Butler & Tanner Ltd, Frome, Somerset

Distributed in the US by Publishers Group West

Published by Sanctuary Publishing Limited, Sanctuary House,
45–53 Sinclair Road, London W14 0NS, United Kingdom

www.sanctuarypublishing.com

Jacket artwork: Caroline Church
Jacket design: Splashdown

Publisher's Note
This book covers a wide range of sports, each with their own preferences and
peculiarities when it comes to units of measurement. In most cases, you will find
that we have followed the preferences and conventions of each particular sport,
so, for example, distances in golf are given in yards, while in athletics they are in
metres. Wherever possible, we provide conversion figures in parentheses after the
original measurement.

ISBN: 1-86074-510-5

Fotheringham's Sporting Trivia

The Greatest Sporting Trivia Book Ever...

Will Fotheringham

Sanctuary

— ACKNOWLEDGEMENTS —

This book could not have been written without the invaluable contribution of my friend and colleague Tim Clifford. His tireless research, endless patience and willingness to travel to the more distant reaches of sport with me made the journey a far more pleasant and memorable one.

I also owe a considerable debt to Nick Mason, formerly of the *Guardian*, for giving me the run of his library, and to Michael Arthur, for his kind assistance; my thanks are also due to Harry Pearson for helpful suggestions, and to my sports editor at the *Guardian*, Ben Clissitt, for his continuing support. At Sanctuary, Chris Harvey steered the book seamlessly through production.

As ever, it is to Caroline, Patrick and Miranda for their forbearance in the face of yet more hours chained to the Mac, that I owe the most.

— ABOUT THE AUTHOR —

Will Fotheringham writes for the *Guardian* and *Observer*, mainly on cycling and rugby. Previous books include *Put Me Back On My Bike: In Search Of Tom Simpson* and *Century Of Cycling: The Classic Races And Legendary Champions*. He lives in Herefordshire with his partner and two children.

— PREFACE —

Loving sport and accumulating information go hand in hand. Put two sports fans together in one place and you have a quiz in the making. But this process is not restricted to men kicking balls around and driving cars very fast: it's part of the wider process of information gathering that is the stuff of modern life.

Our ancestors had less stuff to wade through and it was more directly related to survival. In the infinitely varied modern world, we can bathe in facts, lists, coincidences, in the knowledge that we won't become fatally ill if we forget who scored the winning goal in the World Cup. Probably.

One purpose of this book is to help out in those moments when you feel you have the fact at your fingertips, but can't quite place it, to explore those bits of sport that are familiar, yet unfamiliar: why is the Ryder Cup? Who was Roland Garros?

I had another aim as well. Soccer transfers and tennis tantrums are what make the front pages but sport goes much further into an infinite variety of the arcane, the amusing and the plain bizarre. Taking it as a whole is akin to stepping into Douglas Adams' Total Perspective Vortex: if the bite-size chunks I offer here lead you to further investigation, so much the better.

There remains, of course, the vexed question of when a pastime becomes a sport. That is a matter beyond this book, but once you begin to explore Basque woodchopping, you wonder whether all it lacks to become an Olympic sport is pretty girls with bikinis rather than big men with bigger biceps.

THE RULES OF CRICKET
— (AS EXPLAINED TO A FOREIGNER) —

You have two sides: one out and one in

Each man that's in the side that's in goes out
and when he's out he comes in and the next man
goes in until he's out

When they are all out, the side that's out comes
in and the side that's been in goes out and tries
to get those coming in out

Sometimes you get men still in and not out

When both sides have been in and out including
the 'not outs'

That's the end of the game

Howzat!

— BUM DEAL —

In Article XII, Section A of the Rules And
Regulations Of The American Armsport
Association, the US governing body for
competitive arm wrestling, rule 25 states,
'Round dowel rods will be used for
buttock fouls in sit-down competitions.'

— OLYMPIC OATH —

'We swear that we will take part in the Olympic Games in a spirit of
chivalry, for the honor of our country and for the glory of sport.'

The original Olympic oath, as written by Baron de Coubertin and first
publicly sworn in 1920. 'Country' was later replaced by team and
'swear' by promise. An undertaking to abide by the rules has been
added, as has the following rider, first introduced at Sydney in 2000:

'…committing ourselves to a sport without doping and without drugs.'

— AMERICAN FOOTBALL: NFL RIVAL LEAGUES —

Founded in 1920, the NFL was originally known as the American Professional Football Association but changed its name to the National Football League in 1922. Since its inception, the NFL has had to face challenges from eight rival pro leagues. Only one, the fourth version of the American Football League (1960–69), proved more than a short-lived threat, with the two leagues forming a partnership in 1966.

The most recent challenger, XFL, was created in 2001 by Vince McMahon of WWE wrestling, who promised 'football with attitude'. Initially XFL games were aired on NBC, TNN and UPN television networks but its poor play and cartoonish approach (some players wore nicknames such as He Hate Me on their shirts) proved a ratings failure and the league only lasted one season.

DEFUNCT LEAGUES

American Football League I (1926): Boston Bulldogs, Brooklyn Horsemen, Chicago Bulls, Cleveland Panthers, Los Angeles Wildcats, New York Yankees, Newark Bears, Philadelphia Quakers, Rock Island Independents

American Football League II (1936–37): Boston Shamrocks, New York Yankees, Pittsburgh Americans, Rochester Tigers, Brooklyn Tigers (1936 only), Cleveland Rams (1936 only), Cincinnati Bengals (1937 only), Los Angeles Bulldogs (1937 only)

American Football League III (1940–41): Buffalo Indians, Cincinnati Bengals, Columbus Bullies, Milwaukee Chiefs, New York Yankees (1940) changed name to Americans (1941), Boston Bears (1940 only)

All-America Football Conference (1946–49): Cleveland Browns, Los Angeles Dons, San Francisco 49ers. Brooklyn Dodgers and New York Yankees (both 1946–48) merged to become the Brooklyn-New York Yankees (1949), Buffalo Bisons (1946) renamed Bills (1947–49), Chicago Rockets (1946–48) renamed Hornets (1949), Miami Seahawks (1946) became Baltimore Colts (1947–49)

World Football League (1974–75): The Hawaiians, Philadelphia Bell, Southern California Sun, Birmingham Americans (1974) renamed Vulcans (1975), Chicago Fire (1974) renamed Winds (1975), Detroit Wheels (1974 only), Florida Blazers (1974) became San Antonio Wings (1975), Houston Texans (1974) became Shreveport Steamer (1974–75), Jacksonville Sharks (1974) renamed Express (1975), Memphis Southmen (1974) renamed Grizzlies (1975), New York Stars (1974) became Charlotte Hornets (1975), Portland Storm (1974) renamed Thunder (1975)

United States Football League (1983–85): Birmingham Stallions, Denver Gold, Los Angeles Express, New Jersey Generals, Oakland Invaders, Tampa Bay Bandits, Arizona Wranglers (1983–84) merged with Oklahoma Outlaws (1984 only) to become Arizona Outlaws (1985 only), Boston Breakers (1983) became New Orleans Breakers (1984) then Portland Breakers (1985), Chicago Blitz (1983–84), Houston Gamblers (1984–85), Jacksonville Bulls (1984–85), Memphis Showboats (1984–85), Michigan Panthers (1983–84) merged with Oakland (1985), Philadelphia Stars (1983–84) became Baltimore Stars (1985), Pittsburgh Maulers (1984 only), San Antonio Gunslingers (1984–85), Washington Federals (1983–84) became Orlando Renegades (1985)

XFL (2001): Birmingham Thunderbolts, Chicago Enforcers, Las Vegas Outlaws, Los Angeles Xtreme, Memphis Maniax, New York/New Jersey Hitmen, Orlando Rage, San Francisco Demons

The short-lived Spring Football League (SFL) – which was founded in 2000 by a group of ex-NFL players including Eric Dickerson, Drew Pearson, Bo Jackson and Tommy Dorsett – was not a rival to the NFL but merely an attempt to extend the season. The SFL was to be contested by six teams – Houston Marshals, Los Angeles Dragons, Miami Tropics, San Antonio Matadors, LA Stars and Houston Mavericks. The plan was for a four-game season running from 29 April to 27 May, but disappointing crowds from the start meant that only two games were played before the league fell apart. As a result, two teams, the Stars and the Mavericks, never played at all.

— FAST LANE —

American Francis Lane won the first race of the modern Olympic Games, a qualifying heat for the 100m in Athens in 1896. Lane finished third in the final, which was won by another American, Thomas Burke.

— RONNIE'S RAPIDFIRE 147 —

Ronnie O'Sullivan potted the fastest 147 break in a professional snooker tournament on 21 April 1997, at the World Championships in the Crucible Theatre, Sheffield, England. It took O'Sullivan just 5 minutes and 20 seconds to make his maximum break during a first-round match against Mick Price.

— CRICKET'S FIRST CENTURION —

The first game of cricket for which some scores are known was a match between Kent and All England on 18 June 1744, but the first known scoresheet in existence is of a match between the Duke of Dorset's XI and Wrotham on 31 August 1769. Unfortunately, only the scores of the Duke's XI have survived, so no one knows who won, however the 107 by J Minshull in the Duke's team's second innings is the first century on record.

— 100m RECORDS 1896–2002 —

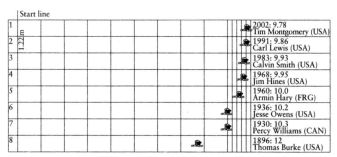

	Start line													
1														2002: 9.78 Tim Montgomery (USA)
2														1991: 9.86 Carl Lewis (USA)
3														1983: 9.93 Calvin Smith (USA)
4														1968: 9.95 Jim Hines (USA)
5														1960: 10.0 Armin Hary (FRG)
6														1936: 10.2 Jesse Owens (USA)
7														1930: 10.3 Percy Williams (CAN)
8														1896: 12 Thomas Burke (USA)

The difference of 2.22 seconds between Burke and Montgomery would give a gap of about 12.3m

— RUNNING A MILE FOR A SHUTTLECOCK —

Each player in a singles badminton match runs 1 mile (1.6km) on average.

— THE MISPLACED APOSTROPHE —

Yachting's America's Cup, it is often assumed, is something to do with the Americas. In fact, it is named after the yacht *America*, which won the original trophy, an ewer presented by the Royal Yacht Squadron for a race around the Isle of Wight. In 1857 the trophy was given to the New York Yacht Club for a perpetual international challenge trophy. *America* was a schooner-rigged yacht of 170 tons designed and built by Steers of New York and financed to the tune of $30,000 (£19,000) by a syndicate.

— THE ASHES —

'In Affectionate Remembrance of English Cricket
Which died at the Oval on 29th August 1882
Deeply lamented by a large circle of sorrowing
Friends and acquaintances.
R.I.P.
NB: The body will be cremated and the ashes taken to Australia'

This mock obituary appeared in the *Sporting Times* after England's first defeat in a cricket Test by Australia; the ashes of a burnt cricket stump were later placed in an urn and given to the England cricket captain, the Hon Ivo Bligh, when his team beat Australia in 1882–83. Hence the nickname given to Test series between England and Australia.

— BATTLE ON THE FOOTBALL FIELD —

The roughest game in NFL history was the battle between the Cleveland Browns and the Chicago Bears on 25 November 1951. Referees awarded penalties on average once every 96 seconds, with the Browns committing 21 infractions for a loss of 209yds and the Bears 16 for a loss of 165yds. In one play, a run of three straight personal fouls by the Browns moved the ball from the Chicago 46-yard line to the Browns 9-yard line. Despite having two players, kicker Horace Gillom and halfback Dopey Phelps, ejected from the field of play, the Browns won the game 42–21.

— KICK-IN GETS THE BOOT —

The throw-in in soccer replaced the kick-in in 1892.

— SIX SIXES FOR SOBERS —

Nottinghamshire's Gary (later Sir Garfield) Sobers scored 36 runs off a single over – bowled by the unfortunate Malcolm Nash – during a match against Glamorgan at Swansea on 31 August 1968. Sobers was caught on the fifth ball by Roger Davis, but the Glamorgan fielder fell over the boundary line. The final delivery was hit clean out of the ground and the ball was not found until the following day. Sobers' feat was emulated on 10 January 1985, by Ravi Shastri playing for Bombay against Baroda in Bombay. On that occasion, Tilak Raj was the bowler to suffer the humiliation of being hit for 36.

— EVERTON, THE ORIGINAL ANFIELD CLUB—

Liverpool FC are forever associated with Anfield, yet the soccer club's arch-rival Everton FC was the first team to play there. Everton FC was founded in 1878 and rented a field in Anfield Road to play its games. A dispute over rent for this ground led to a split in the club, with one faction taking the original name and moving to nearby Goodison Park and the other faction forming a new team, Liverpool Association FC, in 1892.

— CLUBHEAD SPEED —

In a four-round tournament, a professional golfer's clubs will only be in contact with the ball for approximately one-tenth of a second.

— THE FASTEST BALL GAME IN THE WORLD —

The sport of jai alai is reputed to be the fastest ball game in the world. In the Basque region where the game originated, *jai alai* means 'happy festival'. The ball, which is thrown by players using long, curved baskets called chisteras, can reach speeds of 188mph (300kph).

— ONE FALSE MOVE —

A false start was not a good idea at the ancient Olympics. Officials, called *alytes*, would whip offending runners as punishment.

— BBC SPORTS PERSONALITIES OF THE YEAR —

1954	Chris Chataway	Athletics
1955	Gordon Pirie	Athletics
1956	Jim Laker	Cricket
1957	Dai Rees	Golf
1958	Ian Black	Athletics
1959	John Surtees	Formula One
1960	David Broome	Show Jumping
1961	Stirling Moss	Formula One
1962	Anita Lonsbrough	Swimming
1963	Dorothy Hyman	Athletics
1964	Mary Rand	Athletics
1965	Tom Simpson	Cycling
1966	Bobby Moore	Soccer
1967	Henry Cooper	Boxing
1968	David Hemery	Athletics
1969	Ann Jones	Tennis
1970	Henry Cooper	Boxing
1971	Princess Anne	Show Jumping
1972	Mary Peters	Athletics
1973	Jackie Stewart	Formula One
1974	Brendan Foster	Athletics
1975	David Steele	Cricket
1976	John Curry	Figure Skating
1977	Virginia Wade	Tennis
1978	Steve Ovett	Athletics
1979	Sebastian Coe	Athletics
1980	Robin Cousins	Figure Skating
1981	Ian Botham	Cricket
1982	Daley Thompson	Athletics
1983	Steve Cram	Athletics
1984	Torvill & Dean	Ice Dance
1985	Barry McGuigan	Boxing
1986	Nigel Mansell	Formula One
1987	Fatima Whitbread	Athletics
1988	Steve Davis	Snooker
1989	Nick Faldo	Golf
1990	Paul Gascoigne	Soccer
1991	Liz McColgan	Athletics
1992	Nigel Mansell	Formula One
1993	Linford Christie	Athletics

— BBC SPORTS PERSONALITIES OF THE YEAR (CONT'D) —

1994	Damon Hill	Formula One
1995	Jonathan Edwards	Athletics
1996	Damon Hill	Formula One
1997	Greg Rusedski	Tennis
1998	Michael Owen	Soccer
1999	Lennox Lewis	Boxing
2000	Steve Redgrave	Rowing
2001	David Beckham	Soccer
2002	Paula Radcliffe	Athletics

— THE SLOWEST DUCK IN CRICKET HISTORY —

On 2 March 1999, during the first Test between New Zealand and South Africa at Eden Park, Auckland, Geoff Allott recorded the longest innings without scoring in Test history. The New Zealand batsman spent 101 minutes at the crease and faced 77 deliveries before being dismissed without opening his account.

— PITCH PERFECT —

On 8 October 1956, Don Larsen of the New York Yankees pitched the only perfect game ever recorded in baseball's World Series. It took the 6ft 4in (1.93m) right-hander 97 pitches and just two hours and six minutes to retire all 27 of the Brooklyn Dodgers (a team that included such notable sluggers as Jackie Robinson) he faced in the fifth game of the series, which ended with the Yankees winning 2–0 in front of a crowd of 64,519 at Yankee Stadium. Larsen, whose poor performance as starting pitcher in the second game of the series had gifted victory to the Dodgers, was surprised that he was even asked to start the fifth game. His achievement gave the Yankees a 3–2 series lead -- they went on to take the title 4–3 – and earned Larsen the Most Valuable Player of the series award.

— WORLD DWARF GAMES —

The Dwarf Athletic Association of America organised the first international multisports competition for dwarf athletes in Chicago in 1993. Athletes must be shorter than 4ft 10in (1.47m) tall in order to be able to participate in the Games. Sports on the programme include athletics, basketball, weightlifting, boccia (a variant of the Italian bowls game, bocce), swimming, alpine skiing, table tennis, volleyball, badminton, soccer, and equestrian events. The Games are held every four years. Since the inaugural meet, they have been held in Peterborough, England, in 1997 and Toronto, Canada, in 2001. The 2005 Games are scheduled to take place in France.

— BASKETBALL'S ORIGINAL RULES —

Basketball was invented in December 1891 by James Naismith, a Canadian student at a YMCA training college in Springfield, Massachusetts. The game was the product of a homework assignment set by Naismith's PE teacher to devise an indoor winter game for young men. In the original version, peach baskets were nailed to the gym wall to serve as goals and dribbling was not permitted. It wasn't long before dribbling was allowed and hoops replaced baskets. Naismith's original 13 rules follow:

1. The ball may be thrown in any direction with one or both hands.

2. The ball may be batted in any direction with one or both hands (never with the fist).

3. A player cannot run with the ball. The player must throw it from the spot on which he catches it, allowance to be made for a man who catches the ball when running at a good speed if he tries to stop.

4. The ball must be held in or between the hands; the arms or body must not be used for holding it.

5. No shouldering, holding, pushing, tripping, or striking in any way the person of an opponent shall be allowed; the first infringement of this rule by any player shall count as a foul, the second shall disqualify him until the next goal is made, or, if there was evident intent to injure the person, for the whole of the game, with no substitute allowed.

6. A foul is striking at the ball with the fist, violation of Rules 3, 4, and such as described in Rule 5.

7. If either side makes three consecutive fouls, it shall count a goal for the opponents (consecutive means without the opponents in the mean time making a foul).

— BASKETBALL'S ORIGINAL RULES (CONT'D) —

8. A goal shall be made when the ball is thrown or batted from the grounds into the basket and stays there, providing those defending the goal do not touch or disturb the goal. If the ball rests on the edges, and the opponent moves the basket, it shall count as a goal.

9. When the ball goes out of bounds, it shall be thrown into the field of play by the person first touching it. In case of a dispute, the umpire shall throw it straight into the field. The thrower-in is allowed five seconds; if he holds it longer, it shall go to the opponent. If any side persists in delaying the game, the umpire shall call a foul on that side.

10. The umpire shall be judge of the men and shall note the fouls and notify the referee when three consecutive fouls have been made. He shall have power to disqualify men according to Rule 5.

11. The referee shall be judge of the ball and shall decide when the ball is in play, in bounds, to which side it belongs, and shall keep the time. He shall decide when a goal has been made, and keep account of the goals with any other duties that are usually performed by a referee.

12. The time shall be two 15-minute halves, with 5 minutes' rest between.

13. The side making the most goals in that time shall be declared the winner. In case of a draw, the game may, by agreement of the captains, be continued until another goal is made.

— DI STEFANO TAKEN HOSTAGE —

During Real Madrid's 1963 tour of Venezuela, the team's Argentinian winger Alfredo di Stefano was taken hostage by anti-government guerrillas of the FALN. The footballer was released unharmed after two days' captivity.

— 20 BOXERS' NICKNAMES —

Nickname	Boxer
Easton Assassin	Larry Holmes
Brown Bomber	Joe Louis
Manassa Mauler	Jack Dempsey
The Ghost with a Hammer in his Hand	Jimmy Wilde
Bronx Bull	Jake la Motta
Gentleman Jim	James J Corbett
Homicide Hank	Henry Armstrong
Orchid Man	Georges Carpentier

Whitechapel Whirlwind	Jack Kid Berg
Hands of Stone	Roberto Duran
Iron Mike	Mike Tyson
The Hitman	Tommy Hearns
The Bayonne Bleeder	Chuck Wepner
The Golden Boy	Oscar de la Hoya
The Mongoose	Archie Moore
The Living Death	Lew Jenkins
The Wild Bull of the Pampas	Luis Firpo
The Undertaker	Harry Wills
The Boston Tar Baby	Sam Langford
The Black Assassin	Stanley Ketchel

— BANNISTER BREAKS RECORD —

'Ladies and Gentlemen, here is the result of event number nine, the one mile: first, number one, RG Bannister, of the Amateur Athletic Association and formerly of Exeter and Merton Colleges, with a time which is a new meeting and track record, and which subject to ratification will be a new English, British Empire and world record. The time is THREE...'

Norris McWhirter's announcement to the crowd at Oxford's Iffley Road track on 6 May 1954 of Bannister's sub-four-minute mile: the figures '59.4' were drowned out by applause.

— SHAQ'S SIZEABLE SHOES —

The LA Lakers' Shaquille O'Neal, who has been voted Most Valuable Player of the NBA finals three times since 2000, wears size 22 shoes.

ON THEIR BEST BEHAVIOUR:
— THE LADY BYNG MEMORIAL TROPHY —

Ice hockey players are not known for being good sports but this long-standing award recognises just that. Lady Evelyn Byng, wife of Baron Byng of Vimy, the Governor-General of Canada, first presented the trophy that bears her name in 1925 to the hockey player 'adjudged to have exhibited the best type of sportsmanship and gentlemanly conduct combined with a high standard of playing ability'. The inaugural winner was Frank Nighbor of the Ottawa Senators.

ON THEIR BEST BEHAVIOUR:
— THE LADY BYNG MEMORIAL TROPHY (CONT'D) —

After Frank Boucher of the New York Rangers won the award seven times in eight seasons (1928–31, 1933–35), he was given the trophy to keep and Lady Byng donated a new one for the 1936 season. After her death in 1949, the National Hockey League presented a new trophy, changing the name to the Lady Byng Memorial Trophy. In its history, only two defensemen, Bill Quackenbush (Detroit Red Wings, 1949) and Red Kelly (Detroit Red Wings, 1951, 1953–54; Toronto Maple Leafs, 1961) have won the Lady Byng. The winner is now selected in a poll of the Professional Hockey Writers' Association. Leading winners: Frank Boucher (7), Wayne Gretzky (5), Red Kelly (4).

— THE DERBY —

This horseracing classic is named after the English Earl of Derby – who established the race in 1780 at Epsom, Surrey, England. The Earl also founded the Oaks, run the day before the Derby, and named after an estate near Epsom belonging to the Earl, which was called The Oaks. The meeting was first run in 1730, and since then has only been interrupted by the two World Wars. Derby Day was traditionally the first Wednesday in June, but since 1995, when the meeting was shortened from four days to three, the Oaks has been on the Friday, the Derby on Saturday, and the closing events on the Sunday.

— THE FIRST OLYMPIAD —

The Games take their name from the valley of Olympia in the Peloponnese, Greece, not from the mountain Olympus. Olympia was the home of a temple to the Greek god Zeus, which contained the massive statue known as the Olympian Zeus, 60ft (18.3m) high and made of gold and ivory, to which the Games, held every fourth year in July, were dedicated. The Games included racing, wrestling and running, and lasted five days. The first Olympiad began in 776 BC and the last, the 293rd, in AD 392.

— KEEPIE UPPIE —

The current world record of nine hours and six minutes, with a total of 55,187 touches, is held by Milene Domingues, a Brazilian former model who balanced the ball on the back of her neck in order to take toilet and meal breaks. She is also nicknamed Rainha das Embaixadinhas (Queen of Juggling) and is married to Brazil's star striker Ronaldo. In 2002–03 she played for Fiamma Monza in Italy.

— THOSE OTHER GREEK GAMES —

As well as the Olympics, held every fourth year, the ancient Greeks also held the Isthmian Games, in the second and fourth year of each Olympiad in the spring. They were named after their location on the isthmus of Corinth, and included gymnastics, music competitions and horse racing. The Pythian games were held in the third year of each Olympiad, at Pytho, also known as Delphi.

— AINTREE COURSE —

Two circuits, Total 4.5 miles

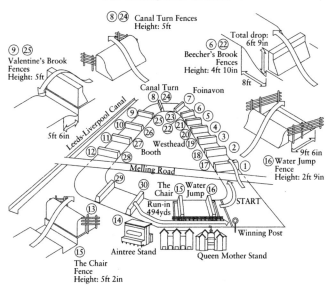

THE TEN FOUNDER MEMBERS
— OF THE SCOTTISH FOOTBALL LEAGUE IN 1890 —

Abercorn *Voted out in 1915*
Cambuslang *Voted out in 1892*
Celtic
Cowlairs *Voted out in 1895*
Dumbarton
Heart of Midlothian
Rangers
St Mirren
Third Lanark *Voted out in 1967*
Vale of Leven *Voted out in 1924*

THE 12 ORIGINAL MEMBERS
OF THE FOOTBALL LEAGUE FROM 1888
— AND WHAT HAPPENED TO THEM IN 2002–03 —

Aston Villa – 16th, Premiership
Blackburn Rovers – 6th, Premiership
Bolton Wanderers – 17th, Premiership
Burnley – 16th, 1st Division
Derby County – 18th, 1st Division
Everton – 7th, Premiership
Notts County – 15th, 2nd Division
Preston North End – 12th, 1st Division
Stoke City – 21st, 1st Division
West Bromwich Albion – 19th, Premiership (relegated)
Wolverhampton Wanderers – 5th, 1st Division (promoted via play-offs)
Accrington Stanley *Resigned from League in 1962*

— THE PERILS OF BULLFIGHTING —

Taurotraumatologia is a specialist branch of medicine found in many Hispanic countries. It deals with injuries typically sustained in the bullring, such as pierced thighs, ruptured rectums and eviscerated scrota.

— THE OLD COURSE AT ST ANDREWS —

Hole	Name	Yards	Par
1	Burn	370	4
2	Dyke	411	4
3	Cartgate (Out)	352	4
4	Ginger Beer	419	4
5	Hole O'Cross (Out)	514	5
6	Heathery (Out)	374	4
7	High (Out)	359	4
8	Short	166	3
9	Hole End	307	4
Out		**3272**	**36**
10	Bobby Jones	318	4
11	High (In)	172	3
12	Heathery (In)	316	4
13	Hole O'Cross (In)	398	4
14	Long	523	5
15	Cartgate (In)	401	4
16	Corner Of The Dyke	351	4
17	Road	461	4
18	Tom Morris	354	4
In		**3294**	**36**
Out		**3272**	**36**
Total		**6566**	**72**

— THE HOLLYWOOD CRICKET CLUB —

Formed in 1932 at Griffith Park, Los Angeles, by C Aubrey Smith, an English character actor who was a former England captain. A stickler for correct behaviour, he once sent Errol Flynn home from a match because his breath smelt of alcohol. Those who have turned out include Basil Rathbone, Nigel Bruce, Boris Karloff, PG Wodehouse and David Niven.

— 1,500M RECORDS —

MEN

Sport	Name	Time	Date	Venue
Speed skating	Derek Parra (USA)	1:43.95	February 2002	Salt Lake City
Running	Hicham El Guerrouj (Morocco)	3:26.00	July 1998	Rome, Italy
Swimming	Grant Hackett (Australia)	14:34.56	July 2001	Fukuoka, Japan

WOMEN

Sport	Name	Time	Date	Venue
Speed skating	Anni Friesinger (Germany)	1:54.02	February 2002	Salt Lake City
Running	Qu Yunxia (China)	3:50.46	September 1993	Beijing, China
Swimming	Janet Evans (USA)	15:52.10	March 1988	Orlando, Florida

— ANCIENT ORIGINS OF GOLF —

1457 'Gouf' is banned for the first time in Scotland by an Act of Parliament. It will be banned again in 1470 and 1491. Football has been banned since 1424.

1527 The Panmure Register describes one Sir Robert Maule as having, 'gryt delight in haukine and hountine... Lykewakes he exercisit the gowf.'

1567 Mary Queen of Scots is attacked for playing golf within two days of the death of her husband, Darnley.

1628 The Marquis of Montrose's accounts show payment of four shillings 'to the boy who carried my clubs'.

1682 First international match. The Duke of York and a shoemaker defeat two English nobles at Leith, Scotland.

1744　First meeting of Honourable Company of Edinburgh Golfers, considered the first golf club in the world.

1754　St Andrews Club is founded; it will later be known as the Royal and Ancient.

— DUTCH MASTER —

'Total football' was the name given to the free-flowing style of football developed by Ajax's coach Rinus Michels in the late 1960s. Michels' tactic of players in constant motion, switching roles to suit the run of play, led the Dutch side to victory in the European Champions Cup in 1971, 1972 and 1973.

— CROSS-CHANNEL SWIMMING —

The first person to swim the English Channel may have been Jean-Marie Saletti, a French soldier who escaped from an English prison hulk in Dover and apparently swam to Boulogne in 1815. It is suspected, though, that he used a raft or small boat to assist his crossing.

Captain Matthew Webb of England made the first authenticated cross-Channel swim. On 24–25 August 1875, he completed the distance from England to France – 20 miles (32km) at its narrowest point, Cap Nez Gris to Dover, although currents and shipping usually add to the swum distance – in 21 hours 45 minutes. As the crawl had not yet been invented, he used a mixture of breaststroke and sidestroke. Webb later drowned trying to swim the rapids above Niagara Falls.

In 1923 Henry Sullivan became the first American to swim the English Channel.

Gertrude Ederle was 19 when she became the first woman to swim the English Channel on 6 August 1926. Her swim from France to England took 14 hours 30 minutes, breaking the existing speed record set by a man. The crew and journalists following her attempt, kept her spirits up by singing 'Yes We Have No Bananas' during the course of the journey.

— CROSS-CHANNEL SWIMMING (CONT'D) —

The record for the fastest cross-Channel swim was set in 1994 by Chad Undeby of the USA, who set out from England and arrived in France 7 hours and 17 minutes later.

Antonio Abertado of Argentina completed the first double swim – from England to France and back – of the Channel in 1961. He spent 43 hours and 10 minutes in the water, with a 5-minute break in France at halfway.

Alison Streeter MBE has swum the Channel more often than anyone else. Her tally, which stood at 39 in 2003, includes a 1990 three-way swim (from England to France and back, then a return to France, which took 34 hours 40 minutes), three two-way swims and 30 single crossings.

The youngest person to complete the swim is Thomas Gregory of Great Britain, who was 11 years and 11 months old when he achieved the feat in 1988 in a time of 11 hours and 54 minutes. The year before, Clifford Batts of Australia became the oldest person – at 67 years and 240 days – to go the distance, swimming it in 18 hours and 37 minutes.

There have been nearly 1,000 successful cross-Channel swims. Less than 7 per cent of efforts succeed.

— RACEHORSE ANCESTRY —

Byerley Turk   Godolphin Barb   Darley Arabian

These are the three stallions imported to England during the 17th and 18th centuries from which all thoroughbred racehorses can trace their ancestry. The Turk arrived in Britain in 1689, after being captured at the siege off Buda three years earlier, and counted among its descendants, Herod, foaled in 1758. The Barb came to Britain from North Africa, known then as Barbary, and was the grand-sire of Matchem, foaled around 1748. The Darley Arabia, imported from Syria by the British consul Thomas Darley, was great-great-grandsire of Eclipse, foaled in 1764. Of the 174 stallions mentioned in 1791 in the first

General Stud Book – the register of thoroughbreds – only the lines of Eclipse, Herod and Matchem have survived. The Darley Arabian has the most successful line: around 80 per cent of modern racehorses can be traced back to him. Ironically, he never actually raced.

— FASTEST SENDING-OFF IN ENGLISH SOCCER —

Sheffield Wednesday 'keeper Kevin Pressman was sent off after just 13 seconds for handling a shot from Wolverhampton's Temuri Ketsbaia outside the area during the opening weekend of the 2003/04 season.

FASTEST MEN IN THE WORLD,
— A BRIEF SELECTION —

Harry Egger (Austria): world speed skiing record holder with 155.6mph (250.4kph), set at Les Arcs in the Alps on 2 May 1999.

Steve Fossett (US): transatlantic sailing record holder, for the west to east course (Ambrose Light, New York to Lizard Point, Cornwall), 4 days, 17 hours, 28 minutes, 6 sec, an average speed of 16mph (25.74kph) in October 2001 in the yacht *Playstation*.

John D Buckstaff (US): ice sailing speed record holder with 230kph (143mph) on Lake Winnebago, Wisconsin in *Debutante* in 1938, apparently with the help of a 72mph (116kph or 63 knot) wind.

Ken Warby (Australia): powerboat, 317.6mph (511.11kph) set on 8 October 1978 in *Spirit of Australia* at Blowering Dam in New South Wales.

Mike Brooke (France): world speed skydiving, 307.15mph (494.20kph) at 'Lille Speed Meet', June 2002, Lille, France.

Greg Rusedski (Canada/UK): fastest tennis serve, 239.78km (149mph), 1998, semi-final at Indian Wells.

Juan-Pablo Montoya (Brazil): fastest ever lap in Formula One, set in qualifying at Monza, Italy, with 161.484mph (259.878kph) on 14 September 2002.

— LONG-DISTANCE INFORMATION —

Equestrian competitors at the 1956 Olympics must rank as the most isolated in the Games' history. Because of Australia's strict quarantine laws, they were forced to compete in Stockholm, Sweden, a city 9,696 miles (15,601km) away from Melbourne, Australia, the host city.

— THE FIRST ETON v HARROW CRICKET MATCH —

This took place in 1805 at Thomas Lord's cricket ground (then on the site of Dorset Square, London). The poet Lord Byron was on the losing Harrow side.

— CHEQUERED LIVES OF SPORT'S GREAT TROPHIES —

The Jules Rimet Cup, awarded to winners of the soccer World Cup, spent the Second World War hidden in a shoebox under the bed of Italian FIFA vice-president Dr Ottorino Barassi to protect it from the Nazis. In March 1966 the trophy was stolen while on display in London but was found a week later wrapped in newspaper under a hedge by a man walking his dog in south London. On 19 December 1983 it was stolen from a display cabinet at the HQ of the Brazilian FA and probably melted down into 4lb (1.8kg) of pure gold.

The FA Cup has been dropped at least twice; first by Charlton manager Jimmy Seed after his team had beaten Burnley 1–0 in the 1947 final, and again after the 1992 final, which Liverpool won 2–0 against Sunderland, when the culprit was the Liverpool coach Phil Thompson.

The America's Cup was badly damaged on 14 March 1997 when Benjamin Peri Nathan smashed it with a sledgehammer, apparently in protest at the New Zealand government's treatment of Maoris. Nathan was sentenced to two years and ten months in jail for the attack and was beaten up several times by fellow inmates outraged at his actions.

The Ryder Cup has been in the wars as well. After the victory party following Europe's 1997 win over America in Valderama, Spain, the gold trophy was dented and had its base hanging off. PGA spokesman Mike Gray commented diplomatically: 'The cup was damaged during the celebrations.'

Ice hockey's Stanley Cup was used as a football by jubilant Ottawa Silver Seven players, who attempted to punt the cup over a frozen local canal in 1905. The following year, members of the Montreal Wanderers took the trophy to a local photographer's studio...but forgot to take it with them when they left. Weeks later, officials discovered the photographer's mother was growing geraniums in it. The Cup has also been left on the roadside, in hotels and, once, in the middle of the rink.

Canadian football's Grey Cup was kidnapped in 1969 from Ottawa's Lansdowne Park. The CFL received a ransom demand for its return but refused to pay it. Police later recovered the trophy from a Toronto hotel. In 1987, the trophy was broken when a member of the victorious Edmonton Eskimoes team sat on it, and in 1993 it was again damaged when another Edmonton player, Blake Dermott, head-butted it. Four years later, kicker Mike Vanderjagt, then of the Toronto Argonauts, left it in a bar in his home town, where it was stolen by college students.

Rugby's venerable Calcutta Cup, fought over annually by England and Scotland, was taken on a drinking spree by the Scotland captain John Jeffrey and the England No8 Dean Richards in 1988 in Edinburgh. No one can quite remember what happened to the cup, save that it needed £1,000 ($1,600) of repair work, and Jeffrey received a six-month playing ban.

— BANDY —

Bandy is a variant of ice hockey, which emerged in the frozen fens of eastern England, when the Bury Fen Bandy Club was founded in the 18th century, 100 years before ice hockey was invented in Canada. Each team has 15 players (including two goalkeepers) of whom 11 have to be on the pitch at any one time. As in soccer, there are two 45-minute halves, penalties, and free strokes following infringements by the other side. The equipment used is similar to that in hockey, but lighter because the speed of bandy ensures there is less physical contact between players. Bandy is played in Canada, the USA, Sweden, Holland, Germany and the former Eastern Bloc.

— HEELS OVERHEAD FOR DA SILVA—

The bicycle kick's first proponent was Leonidas da Silva, a Brazil international of the 1930s.

— LEFT-HANDED BASEBALL PLAYERS —

On 9 August 2002, Barry Bonds of the San Francisco Giants became only the fourth player to hit 600 home runs in his career. Of the four, only Bonds and the legendary Babe Ruth batted left-handed.

TOP LEFT-HANDED HITTERS

Babe Ruth	714 home runs
Barry Bonds	600 home runs
Reggie Jackson	563 home runs
Ted Williams	521 home runs
Willie McCovey	521 home runs

Mickey Mantle hit 536 home runs in his career, but was a switch-hitter.

— BIZARRE SOCCER INJURIES —

Player	Club	Injury
Mo Johnston	Rangers	Strained back

How he did it: Hurled a lump of mud at the pitch after missing an easy chance against Aberdeen

Dave Beasant	Chelsea	Severed tendon in foot

How he did it: Attempted to catch a jar of salad cream as it fell to the ground

Robbie Fowler	Liverpool	Knee strain

How he did it: Stretching to pick up TV remote control

Steve Morrow	Arsenal	Broken arm

How he did it: Dropped when skipper Tony Adams put him over his shoulder during celebrations after 1993 Coca-Cola Cup final

Denis Law	Manchester United	Broken hand

How he did it: Punched the air when Bill Foulkes scored in 1968 European Cup semi-final against Real Madrid, putting his fist through the dug-out roof

Alex Stepney	Manchester United	Dislocated jaw

How he did it: Shouting at team-mates

Santiago Canizares	Valencia	Severed tendon

How he did it: Dropped bottle of eau de cologne on his foot

— BIZARRE HOCKEY RITUAL 1 —

Since April 1952, fans of the Detroit Red Wings have thrown octopuses on to the ice after important wins. The custom began during a Red Wings run in the Stanley Cup when brothers Pete and Jerry Cusimano, who owned a local fish shop, threw an octopus onto the ice during a home game. Back then, eight victories were needed to win the Cup and each tentacle symbolised a Red Wings victory in the play-offs. The largest octopus to be thrown on to the ice was a 50-pounder (22.5kg) in 1996.

— LACROSSE REFEREE CALLS —

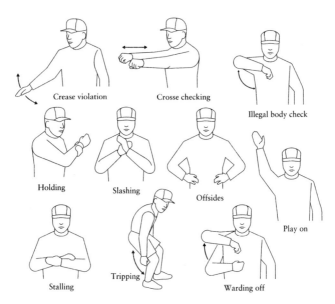

Crease violation

Crosse checking

Illegal body check

Holding

Slashing

Offsides

Play on

Stalling

Tripping

Warding off

— DISCONTINUED OLYMPIC SPORTS —

Standing jumps

While the standing hop, step and jump was only featured twice at the Games – in 1900 and 1904 – there were standing high and long jump contests at every Olympics from 1900 to 1912. Ray Ewry of the USA was the most successful athlete in this field, winning in all three disciplines at the 1900 and 1904 Games and in both the standing long and high jumps in 1908.

56lb (25.4kg) weight throw

This test of strength was contested twice – in 1904 and 1920. Etienne Desmarteau of Canada took top honours on the first occasion, the only non-American to win a track and field event in St Louis. The 1920 winner, Patrick McDonald, was a New York policeman, who tipped the scales at 350lb (158kg).

12-hour cycling
Cycling events have been held at every modern Olympics, but the 1896 Games in Athens was the only one to include a 12-hour race. Winner Adolf Schmal of Austria rode 295.3km (183½ miles) to Frank Keeping of Great Britain's 294.65km (183 miles) – a tight finish given the length of the race and that they were the only two to complete the event.

Live pigeon shooting
One of the more bizarre events at the 1900 Paris Olympics, competitors were eliminated if they missed two birds. Leon de Lunden of Belgium's tally of 21 kills earned him victory in a contest that dispatched over 300 birds in total.

Motor boating
Three categories of powered boat racing – under 60ft (18m), 26ft (8m) and open – were contested at the 1908 Games in London. The first two were won by the British crew (Thomas Thornycroft, Bernard Redwood and Thomas Wynn Weston) of *Gyrinus II*, while France's Emile Thubron in *Camille* won the third. In each race, held over 40 nautical miles, there was only one finisher.

Plunge for distance
Contestants in this event at the 1904 St Louis Games of 1904 executed a standing dive into the swimming pool and then were not allowed to move their bodies for one minute or until they ran out of breath. The length of the dive was then measured. William Dickey's winning plunge of 62½ft (19.05m) led an American clean sweep of the top five places.

Croquet and roque
The lawn game didn't exactly set the world alight when it appeared at the 1900 Paris Games. Only one spectator, an Englishman, paid to witness the contest between two Frenchmen, known only by their surnames Aumoit and Waydelich, with the former taking victory. Roque, a variant of croquet, featured at the St Louis Games in 1904. This competition was won by Charles Jacobus of the USA.

— DISCONTINUED OLYMPIC SPORTS (CONT'D) —

Underwater swimming

This event featured for the first and last time at the Paris Games of 1900. Two points were awarded for each metre swum underwater, and one point was given to each competitor for every second he remained below the surface. Frenchman Charles de Venderville won by swimming 65½yds (60m) and staying submerged for 1min 8.4sec, although Denmark's Peder Lykkeberg stayed underwater for longer but mostly swam in circles and travelled just 31yds (28.3m).

One-handed weightlifting

This was one of the events at the first modern Olympics in 1896 and appeared at both the 1904 – but only as part of as an all-round dumb-bell competition won by Oscar Osthoff of the USA – and 1906 Games, too. The inaugural contest was won by Launceston Elliott of Great Britain, while Josef Steinbach of Austria secured victory at the 1906 Games in Athens.

Cricket

It appeared only once – at the 1900 Paris Olympics – and the winners were Great Britain and in a way so were the losers, because the 'French' team they beat consisted of staff from the British embassy in Paris. Another sport with British origins, rugby, proved a more durable component of the Olympics, featuring in the Games of 1908, 1920 and 1924.

Tug of war

Included between 1900 and 1920, but there was confusion about how many men should make up a team. USA won the first three places in 1904 with five-man teams; Britain did the same in 1908 with nine-man teams. By 1912 eight was the established figure; Britain were the last winners, beating the US in 1920.

— THE TENNIS VOLLEY —

Spencer Gore was the first exponent of the volley – hitting the ball before it bounces – in tennis. He introduced the stroke at the first Wimbledon championships in 1877, which he won.

— OLYMPICK SHINDIG IN GLOUCESTERSHIRE —

Captain Robert Dover, who was in fact a local barrister, inaugurated the Cotswold Olympick Games in 1612. A natural amphitheatre on the outskirts of Chipping Campden, Gloucestershire, was employed as the venue for a number of unusual sports, including shin-kicking, tug of war and obstacle races. The Games have been held annually in Whitsun week ever since.

— THE DUCKWORTH-LEWIS SYSTEM —

This system, which is used to calculate the target for victory in weather-affected one-day cricket matches, was invented by Frank Duckworth (a consultant statistician) and Tony Lewis (a lecturer in mathematics). Based on the principle that teams have two 'resources' available to them in a cricket match: time remaining to match the opposition score; and the wickets in hand to achieve it with. The D/L method calculates a 'resource percentage': for a team with 50 overs (the usual one-day quota) and 10 wickets in hand, it is 100 per cent. Resource percentages are expressed in a table for scorers. If there are stoppages in play and the team batting second have fewer 'resources' available, their target is reduced by a ratio, which is the difference between the team's percentages at the stoppage. If the team batting second have greater 'resources', their target is increased.

Extract from the table of resource percentages remaining
Horizontal scale: Wickets lost Vertical scale: Overs left

	0	2	5	7	9
50	100.0	83.8	49.5	26.5	7.6
40	90.3	77.6	48.3	26.4	7.6
30	77.1	68.2	45.7	26.2	7.6
25	68.7	61.8	43.4	25.9	7.6
20	58.9	54.0	40.0	25.2	7.6
10	34.1	32.5	27.5	20.6	7.5
5	18.4	17.9	16.4	14.0	7.0

— THE STUPIDEST OWN GOAL EVER —

Arsenal left-back Dennis Evans scored one of the most ridiculous goals of all time *for* Blackpool at Highbury in 1955. With a few seconds remaining, Arsenal were 4–0 ahead when Evans heard what he thought was the final whistle and flicked the ball into his own net. The goalkeeper had also thought he had heard referee Frank Coultas blowing up and was gathering his hat and gloves. The whistle had, however, been blown by a spectator.

— TRIPLETS RUN MARATHON —

On 13 April 2003, 27-year-olds Louise, Jane and Vicky Heppner became the first triplets to run the London Marathon.

— CAMEL WRESTLING —

Camel wrestling, pitting animal against animal, is a popular traditional winter sport in Turkey, with the biggest festival taking place at Selçut in the ancient stadium of Ephesus. To prevent mismatches, the organisers pair camels on weight, size and leading foot. Camels, like humans, can be right-footed, left-footed or ambidextrous.

— BOOMERANGS —

The six standard events of boomerang competition:

Accuracy
The competitor throws from a bullseye painted on the ground and is awarded points (maximum 50) based on where the boomerang lands in relation to the bullseye.

Trick Catch
Catches are made with one hand, behind the back, under the leg or with the feet.

Australian Round
A test of distance, accuracy and catching ability. A boomerang with a range of 50m (55yds) gets

maximum distance points. A catch in the bullseye gets maximum accuracy and catching points.

Fast Catch
Using the same boomerang, the competitor makes five throws and catches as quickly as possible.

Maximum Time Aloft
The longest of five throws to stay in the air.

Endurance
This is 'Fast Catch' for five minutes. The competitor who makes the most catches in the time wins. Long-distance throwing is a separate event, held when the space is available.

— BIZARRE HOCKEY RITUAL 2 —

In 1996, Florida Panthers' winger Scott Mellanby was getting ready for a game when a large rat ran through the dressing room. Mellanby killed it with his hockey stick – and went on to score two goals in the game. After that, Panthers fans started throwing plastic rodents on to the ice whenever the team scored. That season, the team progressed to the Stanley Cup finals and the ice would often be covered with rats each time the Panthers scored. The NHL banned the practice after the 1996 season because clearing the ice of rats was delaying games.

— FIRST BASEBALL MATCH —

The basic modern rules of baseball were written in about 1845 by Alexander Cartwright of the New York Knickerbockers, who played the first match according to Cartwright's rules on 19 June 1846 at the Elysian Fields in Hoboken, New Jersey, against the New York Base Ball Club. The match lasted only four innings, as the nine-inning rule had not been adopted, and that was all it took for the New York team to score 21 'aces' as runs were known, which was what was required for victory.

— BOWLING FOR BIG BUCKS —

More than 3 million Americans are members of bowling organisations and ESPN regularly broadcasts professional tournaments on Sunday afternoons. The Professional Bowlers' Association Tour, which runs from September to March, is a lucrative one for those at the top of the game, as this table of earnings for the 2002–03 season shows:

Pos	Name	Events	Earnings
1	Walter Ray Williams Jr	21	$419,700
2	Chris Barnes	22	$183,930
3	Jason Couch	21	$150,470
4	Norm Duke	22	$145,000
5	Bryon Smith	21	$136,700
6	Pete Weber	20	$134,350
7	Lonnie Waliczek	20	$125,720
8	Danny Wiseman	21	$120,150
9	Brian Voss	22	$115,675
10	Ryan Shafer	22	$100,740

When Walter Ray Williams Jr won the US Open in 2003, the 43-year-old from Ocala, Florida, became the first person in bowling history to have earned more than $3 million as a pro. In fact, victory at the PBA world championships in March 2003, took his total career earnings to $3,131,801. Bowling isn't Walter's only speciality – he is also a six-time world horseshoe pitching champion.

— FA CUP IN BRIEF —

• First final: Wanderers beat Royal Engineers 1–0 at the Kennington Oval in London on 16 March 1872. Spectators: 2,000.

• Last amateur winners: Old Etonians in 1882.

• The original FA Cup was stolen from a shop in Birmingham on 11 September 1895 and never returned.

• First monarch to present the Cup: King George V, to Burnley captain Tom Boyle after 1–0 victory v Liverpool at Crystal Palace in 1914.

• First all-ticket final: 1924, between Newcastle and Aston Villa, following a chaotic first Wembley final the year before, when over 200,000 watched Bolton beat West Ham United 2–0.

• Longest unbeaten holders: Portsmouth, winners in 1939. Due to the war, the Cup was not contested again until 1946.

• Longest tie: six games between Alvechurch and Oxford City in fourth qualifying round during November 1975. Commemorative ties were issued to those who could prove they had been to every match.

• Oldest player to appear in final: Billy Hampston, 41 years and 8 months when Newcastle won in 1924.

• Only Welsh winners: Cardiff in 1927, beating Arsenal 1–0.

• Best Scottish club: Queen's Park of Glasgow, finalists in 1884 and 1885, beaten 2–1 and 2–0 by Blackburn Rovers.

• Hat-tricks in final: Billy Townley (Blackburn Rovers, 1890), Jimmy Logan (Notts County, 1894), Stan Mortensen (Blackpool, 1953).

• Record winners: Manchester United, ten victories, as of 2003.

• Youngest captain to win the Cup: Bobby Moore, 23 years 20 days old when he led West Ham to victory over Preston in 1964.

• Biggest winning margin in final: Bury's 6–0 beating of Derby County in 1903 at Crystal Palace

• Biggest winning margin in preliminary rounds: 1888, Preston North End trouncing Hyde 26–0 in the first round.

• Venues: 1872 Kennington Oval
        1973 Lillie Bridge, London
        1874–1892 Kennington Oval
        1893 Fallowfield, Manchester
        1894 Goodison Park
        1895–1914 Crystal Palace
        1915 Old Trafford, Manchester
        1920–22 Stamford Bridge
        1923–2000 Wembley Stadium
        2001– Millennium Stadium, Cardiff

— COLLEGE ALL-STAR GAMES —

In 1934 the *Chicago Tribune* sponsored a pre-season game, which pitted a team of the best university players to have graduated the previous year against the reigning NFL champions. The first Chicago College All-Star game between the Chicago Bears and the All-Stars ended in a scoreless tie.

— COLLEGE ALL-STAR GAMES (CONT'D) —

But it was such a success that the game was held every year from 1933 to 1966 against the NFL champions and from 1967 to 1976 against the Super Bowl champions. When the series was cancelled in 1977, the pros had won 31, lost nine and tied once.

— APPEARANCES IN FA CUP FINALS —

Arsenal 16 • Manchester United 15 • Newcastle United 13 • Everton 12 • Liverpool 12 • Aston Villa 10 • West Bromwich Albion 10

— AMERICAN FOOTBALL POSITIONS —

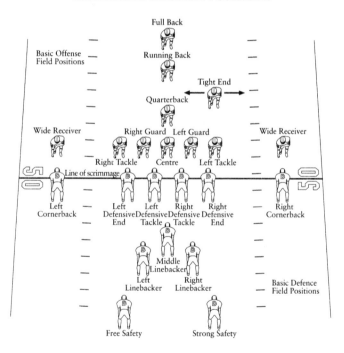

— BOXING WEIGHTS —

Maximum weight	Class
105lb	Minimumweight aka Strawweight or Mini-Flyweight
108lb	Junior Flyweight aka Light Flyweight
112lb	Flyweight
115lb	Junior Bantamweight aka Super Flyweight
119lb	Bantamweight
122lb	Junior Featherweight aka Super Bantamweight
126lb	Featherweight
130lb	Junior Lightweight aka Super Featherweight
135lb	Lightweight
140lb	Junior Welterweight aka Super Lightweight
147lb	Welterweight
154lb	Junior Middleweight aka Super Welterweight
160lb	Middleweight
168lb	Super Middleweight
175lb	Light Heavyweight
190lb	Cruiserweight aka Junior Heavyweight
Over 190lb	Heavyweight

— REWIND AND REPLAY —

CBS was the first television network to use instant replay. It introduced the playback during an Army v Navy American football game on 7 December 1963.

— BRIEF GUIDE TO KABBADI —

The Asian game of Kabbadi is based on teams of 12 players, of whom 7 play. The aim is to score points by sending players into the opposition 'court', which is 21ft by 26ft (6.4m x 7.9m), divided in two. When a player enters the court, this is known as 'a raid'. The 'raider' must begin saying the word 'kabbadi' as he leaves his side, and continue saying it while he is in opposition territory. This is his 'cant'. If he pauses or takes breath during the raid, he is out.

While in the other side's court, he must attempt to touch one or more opponents, or 'antis'. If he manages this, crosses the middle line of their

— BRIEF GUIDE TO KABBADI (CONT'D) —

court (the 'baulk line'), and returns to his side, all the players he has touched are out. On the other hand, if he is caught by the antis and prevented from returning, the raider is out.

Each player a team puts out scores them a point, with a bonus of four points for putting an entire side out. Typically, a match will have halves of 15 or 20 minutes, with teams in five weight categories. Managing a game of kabbadi takes seven officials: referee, two umpires, two linesmen, timekeeper and scorer.

— FOOTBALLERS IN THE DOCK —

In September 1980 Peter Storey, who had been a member of Arsenal's League and Cup double winning side of 1970–71, was sentenced to three years in prison, subsequently reduced to two on appeal, for conspiracy to counterfeit gold half sovereigns.

The entire 32-man Albanian soccer squad were arrested after a shoplifting spree at London's Heathrow airport in May 1990.

In October 1995 Rangers' Duncan Ferguson became the first professional footballer to be jailed for a violent incident on the pitch – he had headbutted John McStay of Raith Rovers – after losing his appeal against a three-month sentence. Prior to his conviction, fans of Glasgow rivals, Celtic, had taunted Ferguson with a terrace chant that ran: 'He's tall, he's skinny, he's going to Barlinnie.' Barlinnie is Scotland's most notorious maximum security prison.

In December 1999, Ipswich Town's player Gary Croft became the first professional footballer to play in a League match while electronically tagged. Wearing the tag was a condition of his early release from prison after he had been jailed for four months for driving while disqualified and attempting to pervert the course of justice.

— A SELECTION OF ARCHERY TERMS —

Anchor: The location to which the hand that draws the bow string is positioned when at full draw.

Anchor point: The place to which an arrow's nock is drawn before release, usually the chin, cheek, ear or chest.

Barrelled: An arrow that is thickest in the middle and tapered to the ends.

Belly of the bow: The surface of the bow closest to the archer when the bow is held in the firing position.

Brace: To string a bow.

Bracer, archer's guard, arm guard: A covering for an archer's wrist designed to protect it from the slap of the string.

Breast: The part of an arrow that touches the bow when the arrow is placed on the string ready to be drawn.

Butt: A target made from compacted straw or an earthen mound used as a backing for such a target.

Cast: The ability of a bow to project an arrow.

Chrysal: A transverse crack in the belly of a wooden bow caused by the crushing of the fibres.

Clout: A white cloth placed on the ground as a marker for long distance shooting.

Clout shoot: An archery contest in which the aim is to hit a target laid horizontally on the ground.

Cock feather: The feather at right angles to the string position in the nock on three feathered arrows.

Compound bow: A modern bow using a system of one or more pulleys to provide mechanical advantage.

Creep: At full draw, to allow the arrow to edge forward just before the moment of release.

Draw: The action of bending the bow to full arrow length by drawing the string backwards while holding the bow steady.

Draw length: The length the bow is drawn to the anchor point.

Draw weight: The force required to draw a bow to full arrow length, usually measured in pounds at a certain draw length measured in inches.

— A SELECTION OF ARCHERY TERMS (CONT'D) —

Feathers: The flights on an arrow that aid stability in flight.

Fistmele: A measurement of the distance from the grip to the string of a bow, usually determined by placing a fist on the grip with the thumb extended towards the bowstring.

Fletcher: An arrow maker.

Fletching: To add feathers to an arrow.

Flemish loose: A loose using two fingers only.

Flight shoot: A distance shooting competition.

Flo: Word of medieval derivation meaning a swift arrow.

Limb: One of the arms of a bow, from grip to tip.

Loose: To release the string of a bow to propel an arrow towards its target.

Mediterranean loose: The three fingered loose used by Western archers.

Mongolian loose: A loose used by archers in Asia whereby the thumb is hooked around the string.

Nock: (1) The end of an arrow with a notch in it for the string. (2) The grooves in the tips of the bow used to fit the bowstring. (3) The fitting of an arrow to the string.

Nocking point: The place on the bowstring where the arrow is placed for firing.

Popinjay: A figure of a bird suspended from a pole that is used as a target.

Recurve bow: A bow where the limbs bend away from the archer when held in the firing position.

Self bow: A bow made out of a single piece of wood.

Sheath of arrows: A bundle of 24 arrows.

Speed shooting, shower shooting: A contest to fire as many arrows as possible into the air at one time.

Spine: A measurement of the amount of elasticity of an arrow shaft.

Tillering: Adjusting the shape, strength or size of a bow.

Toxophily: The love of archery.

Wand shot: An archery contest where the target consists of a piece of peeled willow about 6ft (1.8m) in length placed upright in the ground.

— CLIFF-DIVING —

Cliff-diving was born on the Hawaiian island of Lana'I and the high cliffs at Kaunolu. In 1770, Chief Kahekili was famous for *lele kawa* (jumping off high cliffs and entering the water feet first without splashing). To test his warriors' courage and loyalty, Kahekili forced them to follow his example. A generation later the Hawaiians had turned *lele kawa* into a contest, judged on the style of the dive. Kaunolu remains sacred to the islanders, but *lele kawa* eventually declined and was all but forgotten.

Cliff diving, however, turned into a staple of daredevil shows and TV commercials in the 20th century and the World High Diving Federation was founded in 1996 to establish it as a proper sporting discipline.

Competition divers perform a series of dives judged on technique and style from a platform 23–28m (75–92ft) high for men and 18–23m (59–75ft) for women. Their bodies accelerate to 100kph (62mph) during the three-second fall, then slow to zero as they hit the water, subjecting their bodies to forces of about 100G. The impact is nine times as hard as that when diving off a 10m (33ft) platform. As the WHDF notes: 'It can be assumed that a high diver with experience will not land horizontally. Making a crash-landing into water at 26m (85ft) could be compared to landing on a street at 13m (43ft).'

The WHDF does not permit dives from heights of over 28m (92ft), because the extra acceleration with each added metre of height vastly increases the risk of injury.

2001 WORLD TOUR
Tour competitions took place in Porto Venere, Italy, in Athens, Greece and at Kaunolu, Hawaii.

1.	Orlando Duque	(Col)
2.	Joe Zuber	(Aus)
3.	Peter Bihun	(Aus)

2002 WORLD CHAMPIONSHIP
Brontallo, (Vallemaggia) Switzerland

1.	Orlando Duque	(Col)
2.	Sergey Zotin	(Rus)
3.	Magnus Gardarsson	(Den)

During the opening ceremony of the second Cliff-Diving World Championships in 1998, the Swiss athlete and WHDF founder member Frederic Weill performed a 26m (85ft) armstand forward two-somersaults pike with split dive from a helicopter into Lake Verbano that earned him a place in the Guinness Book of Records.

— SAM SOWS SEEDS OF RYDER CUP —

The Ryder Cup was founded in 1927 by British seed merchant and golf enthusiast Samuel Ryder, who earned a fortune after coming up with the idea of selling seed in small handy packages and was prescribed golf as a cure when he became ill due to overwork. Ryder watched an unofficial US v Britain match at Wentworth in 1926 and came up with the idea of an official tournament, for which he provided a trophy worth £250 ($400). He also had to finance the British team. Sadly, he saw only two Ryder Cups before his death in 1936. Initially the Cup was contested by the US v Great Britain and Ireland, but since 1979 the US has competed against Europe.

— TENNIS GRAND SLAM RECORD HOLDERS —

US tennis player Pete Sampras holds the record for the most men's Grand Slam singles titles. His 14 victories are:

• Australian Open: 1994, 1997
• Wimbledon: 1993–95, 1997–99, 2000
• US Open: 1990, 1993, 1995–96, 2002

He has yet to win the French Open, however.

Australia's Margaret Smith Court holds the women's Grand Slam singles record. Her 24 victories are:

• Australian Open: 1960–66, 1969–71, 1973
• French Open: 1962, 1964, 1969–70, 1973
• Wimbledon: 1964, 1965, 1970
• US Open: 1962, 1965, 1968–70*, 1973

*In 1968 and 1969, the US Open contested both amateur and open championships. Court won the amateur title in 1968 (the open title was won by Britain's Virginia Wade) and both the amateur and open titles in 1969, although records count this as a single title.

— ROCCO BOLTS DOOR ON ITALY'S STRIKERS —

Catenaccio – Italian for 'doorbolt' – is a defensive style of football in which a midfielder slips back to join the defence as a *libero* (free man). Created by Padova coach Nereo Rocco in the early 1950s as a way of countering the goal-scoring abilities of some of the wealthier clubs in Italian league football, it proved so successful that Rocco was hired as coach by one of the rich clubs, AC Milan, taking them to victory in the European Champions Cup in 1963 and 1969. In slang, *catenaccio* can also mean a beaten-up car, which reflects how Italians see the national side when the 'bolt' jams.

— CYCLING HOUR —

Cycling's hour record is just that: the fastest distance a man can cover in an hour...on an oval, banked velodrome. The first man to set a record was the Frenchman Henri Desgrange, who covered 35.325km (21.95 miles) in Paris on 11 May 1893. Ten years later he would go on to organise the first Tour de France. The world governing body, Union Cycliste Internationale (UCI), splits the records up into:

- records set before 1940
- professional records
- amateur records
- records set below 600m (2,000ft) altitude
- records set above 600m (2,000ft), where a speed advantage is gained due to the thinner air.

The UCI recognises two 'absolute' records: a 'world hour record', which is set on a bike without aerodynamic aids, and a 'best hour performance', in which aerodynamic hats and handlebars are allowed. Both are currently held by Chris Boardman of Great Britain.

Best Hour Performance	World Hour Record
56.375km (35 miles)	49.441km (30.72 miles)
6 September 1996	27 October 2000
Manchester	Manchester

— SAM TORRANCE IN FIGURES —

Sam Torrance was the first golfer in
European Tour history to notch up
600 tournaments. He achieved the
milestone at the 1998 Trophée
Lancôme, a month after his 45th
birthday. By then, having spent 28
years on tour, he had walked about
14,000 miles, taken nearly 150,000
shots and earned roughly £1,600
($2,576) per round – or £22 ($35) a
stroke, according to the European
Tour website.

— MOTORCYCLE CATEGORIES —

Category	Power	Weight	Top speed
GP125	45hp	70kg	240kph
GP250	95hp	95kg	270kph
GP500	135–180hp	101–130kg	320kph
Superbike	145–180hp	155–160kg	300kph

*Bikes in the Grand Prix categories are prototypes; Superbikes must be
production models, with a minimum of 500 marketed.*

— GLADIATOR-SPOTTERS' GUIDE —

Samnite: He carries a large oblong shield
(*scutum*) in one hand and a sword
(*gladius*) in the other. On his left leg, he
wears a metal or boiled leather greave
(*ocrea*). On his head, he wears a visored
helmet (*galea*) with a large plumed crest.
The name Samnite derives from a people
defeated by the Greeks in 312 BC.

Thracian: He wears ocrea on both legs
and carries a small square shield. On his
head he wears either a fully-visored
helmet or an open-faced helmet with a

wide brim. His weapon is a curved scimitar (*sica*) or a Thracian sword, which has an angled bend in the blade.

Gallic, also called Murmillo: He carries a rectangular shield and wears a visored helmet decorated with a fish (*murmillo*).

Secutor: A development of the Samnite, the name means 'pursuer'. He fights almost naked apart from an ocrea on his left leg and carries a large oval or rectangular shield. He may be helmetless or wear a round or high-visored helmet. Often, his arms are protected by leather bands at the elbow and wrists (*manicae*). He is traditionally armed with a sword, although occasionally fights with a dagger.

Retiarius: A lightly-armoured gladiator who symbolises the fisherman, he wears only a loincloth (*subligaculum*) and a metal shoulder-piece (*galerus*) on his left arm. He is bare headed and carries a net (*iaculum*) to ensnare his opponents. His weapons include a dagger and a trident or harpoon (*fascina*).

Laquearius: A variation of the retiarius, he carries a lasso instead of a net.

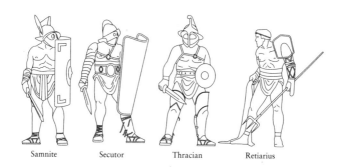

Samnite   Secutor   Thracian   Retiarius

— ORIGINS OF THE RELAY RACE —

Relay racing was not included in the ancient Greek Olympics, even though runners were then used to convey messages from city to city. The idea originated in the late 19th century, when American firefighters ran races in which a red flag was passed between runners every 300m (328yds). The first official relay race was run in Pennsylvania in 1893, and relay events entered the Olympics from 1912.

SOME FORMER NAMES
— OF GREAT ENGLISH SOCCER CLUBS —

First known as	Founded	Became	In
Ardwick FC	1887	Manchester City	1949
Argyle Athletic Club	1886	Plymouth Argyle	1903
Black Arabs	1883*	Bristol Rovers	1898
Dial Square	1886	Arsenal**	1913
Headington United	1896	Oxford United	1960
Newton Heath	1880	Manchester United	1902
Riverside	1899	Cardiff City	1910
Singers	1883	Coventry City	1898
Small Heath Alliance	1875***	Birmingham City	1905
St Jude's	1885	Queen's Park Rangers	1887

   * *Became Eastville Rovers in 1887*

  ** *Royal Arsenal in 1891, Woolwich Arsenal in 1896, Arsenal from 1913*

*** *Dropped the 'Alliance' in 1888*

— HIGHLAND GAMES DISCIPLINES —

The Caber Toss

A caber is a wooden pole weighing 100–150lb (45–68kg) and measuring 18–22ft (5.5–6.7m) in length. The caber is lifted and balanced against the thrower's shoulder. The thrower then runs with it and tosses it end over end. The toss is scored on accuracy, not distance: the thrower attempts to flip the caber completely over so that it lands at 90 degrees to the ground, with the end he was holding at the top. On a clock face this would be 12 o'clock ('pulling a nooner') and is considered the perfect throw.

Weight Toss
A 56lb (25.4kg) weight similar to the one thrown for distance is thrown over a bar with one hand. The thrower stands with his back to the bar and usually takes a few swings to build momentum before releasing the weight. Height is not everything with this event, and the trick is to make the weight curl over the bar so that it does not come straight down.

Weight Throws
The weights used for this event are either 28lb (12.7kg) or 56lb (25.4kg) and are thrown for distance. From behind a wooden board known as the 'trig', the thrower turns, holding the weight in one hand, in similar style to the discus throw. Each thrower has three attempts. Contestants are not allowed to step on or past the trig or the throw does not count.

Scottish Hammer
The Scottish hammer is a round metal ball, either 16lb (7.25kg) or 22lb (10kg) in weight, which is attached to a cane handle. The thrower digs blades on the front of his boots into the ground to have a firm foundation for the throw. With his back facing the direction he wants to throw, the thrower whirls the hammer around his head to build momentum before releasing.

Stone Put
There are two events involving stones. The open stone is similar to the modern shot put with usually a 17lb (7.7kg) rounded stone. The throwers glide or spin to gain momentum for an explosive release. In the Braemar Put (also known as the standing style stone put), a 25lb (11.3kg) stone is thrown from a standing position from behind the trig. This event is more of a test of brute strength than technique.

Sheaf Toss
The thrower stands with his back to a bar and uses a pitchfork to toss a 16lb (7.25kg) or 20lb (9kg) bag of hay or similar material over the bar. The greatest height wins.

— BALL DIMENSIONS —

 Baseball   2¾in (6.985cm) diameter

 Basketball   30–31in (76.2–78.7cm) circumference
= 24.27–25.06cm diameter

 Bowls (wood)   12.1–13cm diameter

 Cricket   8–9in (20.32–22.86cm) circumference
= 6.47–7.28cm diameter

 Croquet   3⅝in (9.21cm) diameter

 Field hockey   7.3–7.7cm diameter

 Football   27–28in (68.58–71.12cm) circumference
= 21.84–22.65cm diameter

 Golf   1⅔in (4.27cm) diameter

 Lacrosse   7¾–8in (19.69–20.32cm) diameter

 Netball   14in (35.56cm) circumference
= 11.32cm diameter

 Polo   3¼in (8.26cm) diameter

 Snooker   2¹⁄₁₆in (5.24cm) diameter

Squash   39.5–40.5mm diameter

◯	Table tennis	38.2mm diameter
◯	Tennis	2½–2⅝in (6.35–6.67cm) diameter
◯	Volleyball	65–67cm circumference = 20.7–21.34cm diameter

Some rules stipulate ball size in inches. These have been converted at 1in = 2.54cm and the metric conversion figures put in brackets. Other rules stipulate ball size by circumference. Diameters for these have been worked out by dividing the circumference by 3.14 (Pi).

— BRIEF GUIDE TO KAZAKH HORSE GAMES —

Horses play a key role in the culture of the Kazakhs of central Asia, who for centuries led a pastoral nomadic existence. Games that display their horsemanship are an important part of every Kazakh festival and celebration.

Kokpar: The two teams try to snatch a goat's carcass and bring it to their half of the field outside a special line. The more times the team brings the carcass outside the special line the more points they get.

Kyz kuu: The horseman attempts to overtake a girl galloping away at full speed with a handicap of 200m (219yds). If the horseman manages it, he is permitted to kiss her. If he fails, the girl attempts to overtake him as he gallops away and is permitted to whip him.

Audyryspak: Two horsemen wrestle in an attempt to push each other out of the saddle.

Kumys-alu: At the gallop, a horseman tries to collect silver coins, which have been scattered on the ground. The most skilful rider gets to keep all the coins.

— FOOTBALL'S NINETY-TWO CLUB —

The Ninety-Two Club is for football
fans who have visited all of the 92
English Football League grounds to
watch a live fixture, with friendlies
and testimonials not counting. The
process can take years – although one
BBC radio commentator attempted to
do all 92 in the 2002–03 season.

— DON BRADMAN PROFILE —

Born: 27 August 1908, Cootamnundra, New South Wales
Died: 25 February 2001, Kensington Park, Adelaide
Test debut: Australia v England at Brisbane, 1st Test, 1928/29
Final test: Australia v England at The Oval, London,
      5th Test, 1948
Tests: 52
Innings: 80
Not-out: 10
Runs: 6,996
Average: 99.94
Test centuries: 29
First-class centuries: 117
Over 200: 37
Over 300: 6
Highest score: 452 not out for New South Wales v
      Queensland, Sydney, 1930
Captained Australia: 24 times (won 15, drew 6 and lost 3)

— GOLF CLUBS AND NUMBERS —

Woods
No1: driver
No2: brassie
No3: spoon
No4: baffy
No5: alternative to No3 or 4 iron

Irons
No1: driving iron
No2: mid-iron
No3: mid-mashie
No4: mashie iron
No5: mashie
No6: spade mashie
No7: mashie-niblick
No8: pitching niblick
No9: niblick
No10: wedge
No number: putter

— HOCKEY'S WORST DEFEAT —

In the 1940s, it was customary for NHL teams to suit up only one goaltender for each game. New York Rangers minder Ken 'Tubby' McAuley probably didn't mind about that as he took to the ice for the Rangers' game against the Detroit Red Wings on 23 January 1944. Although the team was doing so badly that the night before Rangers general manager Lester Patrick had remarked, 'We've got nothing to hope for this season, except for it to end,' McAuley had grounds for cautious optimism. In their previous game, the rookie's goalminding had been widely praised in the press as the Rangers secured an upset, winning 5–1 over the Toronto Maple Leafs.

But within 2 minutes 48 seconds of the opening face-off, the Red Wings scored their first goal and over the course of the next 60 minutes proceeded to put a further 14 into the Rangers net – all of them past McAuley – to complete a 15–0 rout, the biggest defeat in NHL history.

In all, ten Detroit players hit the target, with only defenseman Cully Simon and goaltender Connie Dion staying off the scoresheet.

The Rangers went into freefall after the loss. They did not win again that year until 11 November, an abysmal 0–21–4 record. Among those losses were two further humiliations at the hands of Detroit, who beat them 12–2 on 3 February, and 8–3 on 10 February. Amazingly, McAuley remained in goal, too, eventually playing 96 games for the Rangers. If there hadn't been a war on, no doubt he – and the rest of the team – would have been replaced earlier.

— FAMILY AFFAIRS —

Fathers and sons who have played in a football World Cup

1934 Martin Vantoira (Spain)	1970 Jose Vantoira (Mexico)
1934 Roger Rio (France)	1978 Patrice Rio (France)
1938 Domingos Da Guia (Brazil)	1974 Ademir Da Guia (Brazil)
1950 Mario Perez Sr (Mexico)	1970 Mario Perez Jr (Mexico)
1950 Vicente Asensi (Spain)	1978 Juan Manuel Asensi (Spain)
1962 Cesare Maldini (Italy)	1990–2002 Paolo Maldini (Italy)
1966 Manuel Sanchis Sr (Spain)	1990 Manuel Sanchis Jr (Spain)
1966 Jean Djorkaeff (France)	1998–2002 Youri Djorkaeff (France)
1978 Anders Linderoth (Sweden)	2002 Tobias Linderoth (Sweden)
1986 Cha Bum-Kun (S Korea)	2002 Cha Doo-Ri (S Korea)

— THREE EVENTS FROM THE INUIT GAMES —

The Inuit or Arctic Winter Games are held every two years, and will next take place in 2004 in Fort McMurray, Canada. Participants from Alaska, Yukon, the Northern Territories, Northern Alberta, Greenland and Nunavut compete in a variety of both mainstream and traditional Inuit sports. These are the rules for three of them:

AIRPLANE RULES

1. Start: The player begins lying face down on the floor, legs and feet together, arms extended straight out at right angles to the body and the body firm and rigid. Shoulders should be in line with the starting line. Competitors must maintain a locked arm position with the body remaining above the wrists. This locked position may be at an angle not to exceed 45 degrees at the elbow.

2. Movement: Three assistants, designated by the Head Official, lift the player 2–3ft (60–90cm) above the floor, one grasping the player by the top of each foot and one by each fist. The competitor must remain rigid and fully extended with shoulders and torso supported by the downward pressure of the fists and feet. The player is carried in this position over the pre-set course. The same three assistants will carry each competitor over the course at the same pace. A pacer shall be used to ensure a consistent pace is maintained by the assistants for each competitor. The same pacer shall be used for all competitors.

3. Attempts: Each player is allowed one attempt only.

4. Scoring: The competitor shall be carried over the pre-set course. A player shall be stopped when, in the opinion of the Head Official, the body of the competitor sags below the arms, or the buttocks rise above the arms, or the arms bend at the elbows beyond 45 degrees. The player carried the longest distance will be declared the winner.

5. Competition Format: The order of the players will be established by draw. The course will be pre-set.

6. Course: The course will be pre-set, marked and measured. The course layout should avoid sharp corners. Host officials will attempt to keep the area clean of debris and moisture but it is the athletes' responsibility to ensure the area is safe.

HEAD PULL RULES

1. Start: Two players lie on the floor on their stomachs facing each other. A centre line is drawn between the competitors and two additional lines from the centre line. A looped leather thong or belt is placed over the back of the players' heads above the ears.

2. Movement: Players raise to a 'push-up' position with only hands and feet touching the floor and on signal from one of the judges, pull with their head, bracing their hands out in front and using their whole body strength to pull steadily backward. The pull must be directly back and parallel to the ground. The object is to clearly put the opponent over the line parallel to the centre line.

3. Attempts: This competition consists of one 'pull' to determine a winner.

4. Scoring: The winner of the 'pull' is declared if the opponents hands cross the line, or if the opponent drops his head allowing the loop to be pulled off, or if any part of the body, other than the hands and feet, touches the floor.

5. Competition Format: Double elimination. Initial pairs determined by draw.

6. Equipment: A looped leather thong or belt is used. It is approximately 3ft (90cm) long and 1½in (3.75cm) wide.

— THREE EVENTS FROM THE INUIT GAMES (CONT'D) —

KNUCKLE HOP RULES

1. Start: A player starts face down on the floor in a push-up position with straight legs, elbows bent at the sides of the body and not at an angle away from the body, resting on the knuckles of the hands which are clenched into a fist.

2. Movement: Lifting the body off the floor, then with a quick push of the knuckles and toes, the player hops forward landing again on both knuckles and toes simultaneously. The body must remain off the floor and is extended upward with each hop to the height of the elbows with the buttocks not to extend above the plane of the body.

3. Attempts: Each player is allowed one attempt only.

4. Scoring: The distance the competitor can hop before quitting or lowering his body to the floor is measured from the knuckles at the start to the position of the knuckles at the completion.

A player will be verbally warned if, in the opinion of the judge, the body angle is too high for proper form. A player will be disqualified if he does not correct his form as directed.

The player who hops the longest distance will be declared the winner.

5. Competition Format: The order of the players will be established by draw.

6. Course: The course will be pre-set, marked and measured. The course layout should avoid sharp corners and can be the same as used for the Airplane event.

— JUMPING BOB BEAMON —

Bob Beamon's long jump distance of 29ft 2½in (8.9m) set on 18 October 1968 in Mexico City remains the longest-standing Olympic record. The American was assisted by the thin air at high altitude, but he still added 21¾in (55cm) to the previous distance, and became the first man to beat 28ft (8.5m). But he nearly didn't make the final, as his first two qualifying attempts were 'no jumps'.

— HIT SOCCER SONGS OF THE 1970s —

'Back Home'	England World Cup Squad	No1	June 1970
'Good Old Arsenal'	Arsenal First Team	No16	June 1971
'Blue Is The Colour'	Chelsea	No5	April 1972
'Leeds United'	Leeds United	No10	May 1972
'Nice One Cyril'	The Cockerel Chorus	No14	April 1973
'I'm Forever Blowing Bubbles'	West Ham Cup Squad	No31	May 1975
'We Can Do It'	Liverpool	No15	June 1977
'We've Got The Whole World In Our Hands'	Nottingham Forest and Paper Lace	No24	March 1978

— POLE VAULT —

No outdoor track and field event has seen its world record broken more frequently than the men's pole vault. The record was broken 20 times between 1981 and 2001. Seventeen of the records were set by the great Russian Sergey Bubka.

PRESIDENTS OF THE — INTERNATIONAL OLYMPIC COMMITTEE —

The International Olympic Committee (IOC) was founded on 23 June 1894 by the French educator Baron Pierre de Coubertin who wished to revive the Olympic Games of Greek antiquity. The IOC's president is now widely regarded as the most powerful man in world sport.

Demetrius Vikelas (Greece)   **1894–96**

An educationalist who had no particular connection with sport when he came to Paris to represent the Pan-Hellenic Gymnastic Club at the 1894 Congress that founded the IOC. After the conclusion of the first Games in Athens in 1896, he devoted himself to the promotion of education in Greece, wrote a scholarly work on Byzantine and modern Greece and a couple more whimsical books, *Louki Laras* and *Tales From The Aegean*.

PRESIDENTS OF THE
— INTERNATIONAL OLYMPIC COMMITTEE (CONT'D) —

Baron Pierre de Coubertin (France)   **1896–1925**
The prime mover of the modern Olympic movement, Pierre de Frédy, Baron de Coubertin, left the army at 25, abandoning a promising political career too, in order to devote his energies to his dream of reviving the ancient Olympics. In accordance with his last wishes, after his death in 1937 his heart was interred at Olympia, Greece, in the marble monument commemorating the successful revival of the Games.

Count Henri de Baillet-Latour (Belgium)   **1925–42**
As an IOC committee member, he lobbied for the VII Olympiad to be held in Antwerp in 1920, even though he had only one year to organise the Games and despite the fact that Belgium had been decimated by the First World War. During his presidency, he devoted himself to maintaining the Olympic ideals keeping sport free from all commercialism to preserve its nobility and beauty.

Office vacant   **1942–46**

J Sigfried Edström (Sweden)   **1946–52**
While a student in Gothenburg, Sweden, J Sigfrid Edström was an athlete and ran the 100m in 11 seconds. As an IOC committee member living in a neutral country, he managed to keep in contact with other members throughout the Second World War, and in 1945 convened the first post-war meeting of the Executive Board, which accepted the invitation from London to stage the Games of the XIV Olympiad.

Avery Brundage (USA)   **1952–72**
A talented athlete, who represented the USA at the 1912 Games in Stockholm, Brundage went on to combine a successful career in civil engineering with leading roles in sports administration, first at home then internationally. During his many travels, he amassed one of the finest collections of Asian art in the world. Estimated to be worth $50 million (£31 million), this collection was donated to the city of San Francisco, which built a museum to house it in Golden Gate Park.

Lord Michael Killanin (Ireland)   **1972–80**
Educated at Eton and Magdalene College, Cambridge, Lord Killanin was an accomplished boxer, rower and horse rider in his youth, who went on to find fame as a journalist, especially as a war correspondent in China. He joined the British army at the outset of the Second World War and took part in the Allied landing in Normandy. An IOC member from 1952, he was also the producer of many successful films, including *The Quiet Man* on which he worked with his longstanding friend, John Ford.

Juan Antonio Samaranch (Spain)   **1980–2001**
Samaranch's path to the top of the Olympic movement had an unusual beginning – roller-skating; he led the Spanish team to the world title. Elected as an IOC member in 1966, at the same time he forged a career as a diplomat and served as Spain's ambassador to Moscow from 1977 to 1980. His close contacts with numerous heads of state helped secure the IOC's status as an international non-governmental organisation. He also built up the IOC's finances through television rights and sponsorships.

Jacques Roggé (Belgium)   **2001–**
An orthopaedic surgeon by profession, Roggé competed as a yachtsman at the Games in Mexico in 1968, Munich in 1972 and Montreal in 1976. He was also a member of the Belgian national rugby team.

— TRAMPOLINE —

The trampoline took its name from a pair of Italian trapeze artists, the Due Trampoline, who would bounce on their safety net after performances.

— HAXEY HOOD GAME —

This is played in January each year in the village of Haxey, Lincolnshire. It is a variant of medieval football in which a canvas hood is thrown to the crowd, all of whom attempt to grab it and take it to the nearest pub, eluding 12 colourfully clad players known as 'Boggons'. Twelve canvas hoods are thrown, after which comes a leather one, and after this has been taken to an inn, the game is over. Said to have originated in the 13th century when the hood of a local aristocrat, Lady de Mowbray, blew away as she returned home from church, and was retrieved by 12 labourers.

— THE FA IS BORN...IN A PUB —

Clubs represented at the first meeting of the Football Association in Freemasons' Tavern, Great Queen Street, Lincoln's Inn Fields, London on 26 October 1863.

Charterhouse	Perceval House, Blackheath
No Names, Kilburn	Crystal Palace
Barnes	Blackheath
War Office	Kensington School
Crusaders	Surbiton
Forest (Leytonstone)	Blackheath Proprietory School

The meeting was adjourned, but would eventually lead to the adoption of the rules, which were to be the foundation of soccer in its present form. Crystal Palace were not related to the present club of the same name.

— COMPULSORY ICE DANCE —

Dances recognised by the International Skating Union, two of which must be chosen for the compulsory section of ice dance championships:

Foxtrot	Rumba	European waltz
Rocker foxtrot	14 steps	American waltz
Kilian	Harris tango	Westminster waltz
Yankee Polka	Argentine tango	Viennese waltz
Quickstep	Tango romantica	Starlight waltz
Paso doble	Blues	Ravensberger waltz

— SKI JUMPING STYLE CRITERIA —

Precision
Control during take-off
Position in flight
Position on landing
Position while decelerating

— THE BARD AND HIS BALLS —

'We are glad the Dauphin is so pleasant with us;
His present and your pains we thank you for:
When we have match'd our rackets to these balls
We will, in France, by God's grace play a set
Shall strike his father's crown into the hazard.'

Shakespeare's Henry V expresses his thanks to the Crown Prince of France for his gift of tennis balls prior to the war between England and France.

— TOUR DE FRANCE…TOUR DE PAIN —

'You know how bad you feel when you have flu, how all you want to do is lie in bed?' asked one Tour de France cyclist. 'Well, imagine being made to run upstairs with the flu until you throw up. That's what it's like in the last week of the Tour.' All endurance sport is about withstanding physical pain, but the Tour takes suffering into a new dimension.

The daily menu is 100–125 miles (160–200km), across all terrains, in snow or baking heat, every day for three weeks and 2,500 miles (4,000km). An average speed can be as high as 30mph (50kph) – as good as a small car on the backroads of France. In the Pyrenees and the Alps, the suffering is prolonged, up to an hour's riding up hill at walking pace. The rider passes the height of Ben Nevis from bottom to top, before whizzing down at 60mph (100kph), with death just one miscalculation away. Four or five passes in what can be an eight-hour day in the saddle, with oxygen masks waiting at the top of the day's final mountain – just in case.

It is the realm of the 'toasted greyhounds', men of anorexic fat levels, with hearts that beat fast enough to make the average man keel over, and guts that can process twice as much food as usual. When they struggle into Paris after three weeks, their elbows and hips are covered in 'road rash', their crutches are rubbed raw from days in the saddle, and they are 'too tired to sleep'.

Leanest and meanest of them all is the American hero Lance Armstrong. Just six and a half years ago, he was lying in hospital coughing out chemotherapy poison as he recovered from life-threatening testicular cancer. The treatment for cancer in his brain, lungs and stomach left him with scars on his skull, a catheter in his chest, barely able to cycle to the shops. But he recovered and made a remarkable comeback, winning the Tour four years in a row, 1999–2002. As Armstrong says, after cancer, that puts even the pain of the Tour into perspective.

— NFL NEWCOMERS GO FOR ZERO —

The Tampa Bay Buccaneers had the worst start of any new NFL franchise. When they joined the league in 1976, they lost their first 26 regular season games, scoring no points in 11 of them. Fans became so accustomed to defeat that they began to turn up wearing 'Go for 0' T-shirts. The team finally broke its sustained losing streak on 11 December 1977, when they beat the New Orleans Saints 33–14.

— JESSE OWENS' MAGIC 45 MINUTES... —

... came between 3:15pm and 4pm on 25 May 1935 at the Big Ten inter-collegiate championships at Ann Arbor, Michigan. In spite of a strained back sustained while playing touch football, the athlete who would go on to take four gold medals at the Berlin Olympics 14 months later, persuaded his coach Larry Snyder to let him run the 100 yards. In that event he equalled the world record of 9.4 seconds – in fact, he was probably under it, as in those days timing was by hand and the judges rounded up the figure – and in the next 60 minutes went on to set three further world records. It was the first time any athlete had set multiple world records in track and field events on the same day.

3:15pm	100-yard dash	9.4 sec
3:29pm	long jump	26ft 8¼in
3:40pm	220 yards	20.3 sec
4pm	220-yard hurdles	22.6 sec

Owens' long-jump record remains the longest-standing men's world record of all time. It would not be broken until 12 August 1960.

— WHEN THE TOUR LEFT FRANCE —

Even though the world's greatest cycle race is France's premier sports event, it regularly makes trips abroad, visiting all France's European neighbours, particularly Belgium, which hosted stages almost every year from 1947 to 1982. Even Luxembourg and Andorra have seen stage starts and finishes. Britain was visited in 1974 and 1994, while Ireland hosted three stages in 1998. Starts have also been proposed in Denmark, Canada, the USA and the French West Indies, but remain on the drawing board.

— THE FIRST NEW YORK MARATHON —

In 1970 Gary Muhrcke won the first New York marathon with a time of 2:31.38. That race featured 127 runners; the race now attracts 32,000 and the course record, set by Ethiopia's Tesfaye Jifar in 2001, stands at 2:07.43.

— MUHAMMAD ALI TITLE FIGHTS —

Date/Opponent	Venue	Result	Round
25 February 1964 Sonny Liston	Miami	won (ret'd)	6th
15 May 1965 Sonny Liston	Lewiston	won (knockout)	1st
22 November 1965 Floyd Patterson	Las Vegas	won (stop)	12th
29 March 1966 George Chuvalo (Can)	Toronto	won (points)	15th
21 May 1966 Henry Cooper (Eng)	London	won (stop)	6th
8 August 1966 Brian London (Eng)	London	won (knockout)	3rd
10 September 1966 Karl Mildenberger (Ger)	Frankfurt	won (stop)	12th
14 November 1966 Cleveland Williams	Houston	won (stop)	3rd
6 February 1967 Ernie Terrell	Houston	won (points)	15th

— MUHAMMAD ALI TITLE FIGHTS (CONT'D) —

Date/Opponent	Venue	Result	Round
23 March 1967 Zora Folley	New York	won (knockout)	7th
8 March 1971 Joe Frazier	New York	lost (points)	15th
30 October 1974 George Foreman	Zaire	won (knockout)	7th
24 March 1975 Chuck Wepner	Cleveland	won (stop)	15th
16 May 1975 Ron Lyle	Las Vegas	won (stop)	11th
1 July 1975 Joe Bugner (Eng)	Malaysia	won (points)	15th
1 October 1975 Joe Frazier	Manila	won (ret'd)	14th
20 February 1976 Jean-Pierre Coopman (Bel)	Puerto Rico	won (knockout)	5th
30 April 1976 Jimmy Young	Maryland	won (points)	15th
24 May 1976 Richard Dunn (Eng)	Munich	won (knockout	5th
28 September 1976 Ken Norton	New York	won (points)	15th
16 May 1977 Alfredo Evangelista (Sp)	Landover	won (points)	15th
29 September 1977 Ernie Shavers	New York	won (points)	15th
2 February 1978 Leon Spinks	Las Vegas	lost (points)	15th
15 September 1978 Leon Spinks	New Orleans	won (points)	15th
2 October 1980 Larry Holmes	Las Vegas	lost (ret'd)	10th

Note: all opponents American except where specifically stated.

— LONDON BOASTS LONGEST GAMES —

Recent Olympics have crowded all competitions into a two-week schedule, but activities took place at a more leisurely pace when the Games were revived in 1896. The first Games in Athens, Greece, may have lasted just ten days from 6–15 April, but the second in Paris, France, ran from 20 May to 28 October 1900, a total of 161 days. The most protracted Games of all, though, was the fourth Olympiad in London, England, which began on 27 May and ended 187 days later on 31 October 1908.

— THE ORIGINS OF GOLF TERMS —

The **birdie** was apparently born in 1899, at Atlantic City, New Jersey, according to a story told by Ab Smith, and reproduced in the *Guinness Book Of Golf Facts And Figures* of 1980. 'The second hole was a par 4 about 350 yards long. I was playing in a three-ball match with George A Crump and my brother William P Smith...I banged away with my second shot and my ball came to rest within six inches of the cup. I said "that was a bird of a shot and here I only get a paltry sum from each of you. Hereafter I suggest that when one of us plays a shot in one under par he receive double compensation..." The other two agreed and we began right away to call it a "birdie".'

The logic behind 'eagle' and 'albatross', therefore, is that these birds are rarer than the average birdie.

The **bogey** is said to have originated in 1890, when one Dr Thomas Browne, secretary of the Great Yarmouth club in eastern England, was playing a match against a certain Major Wellman, the match being against the 'ground score', that is the scratch value designated by the club for each hole. The major apparently had not played under this system, and exclaimed that the ground score was a 'bogey man' – that is, a fearsome thing, which only existed in someone's imagination.

The term **caddie** is derived from the French word 'cadet', used for a junior military officer. When Mary Queen of Scots, a keen golfer, returned from France to Scotland, several young officers of this rank formed part of her retinue. It's not known whether they carried the royal

— THE ORIGINS OF GOLF TERMS (CONT'D) —

clubs, but in the 18th century the word came to be used by the Scots to refer to a porter or errand boy, hence its use in golf today. Andrew Dickson was the first caddie whose name we know. He is recorded in 1681 and 1682 as carrying the clubs for the Duke of York, later King James II of England, Scotland and Ireland.

Links – from the old English, *hlinc* (meaning ledge) – is a term that was used in Scotland in the past to describe a strip of land on the sea coast, with sand dunes and grass; areas such as these were used as early golf courses. Sheep inadvertently created the first bunkers by hollowing out holes in the dunes to protect themselves from the wind.

The stymie occurred when one player's ball landed on the green in a position where it would block the other's line to the hole, provided the balls were not within 6in (15cm) of each other. A player was 'stymied', and had no option but to attempt to flick his ball over his opponents, or curve the ball. The Royal and Ancient and US Golf Association abolished the rule in 1952.

Dormie – from the French verb *dormir* (meaning to sleep). The effect of being 'dormie' is that you can sleep easily in the knowledge you cannot be beaten.

Fore – from the 16th-century military command 'beware before', used to warn troops to fall to the ground so that guns could be fired from behind them. It now warns of something similar on golf courses the world over.

Par – According to various wits, can stand for, 'Pretty average really'.

— US AND CANADA MAKE CRICKET HISTORY —

For all that England is regarded as the home of cricket, it did not figure in the first international cricket match. That was played between Canada and the US at St George's Cricket Club, Manhattan. Canada won by 23 runs, batting first and scoring 82 and 63 to the US's 64 and 58. The match fee was $1,000 (£620) per side.

— GREAT MILER'S NICKNAMES —

Walter George Britain	4:12.75	1886	The Wiltshire Wonder
Paavo Nurni Finland	4:10.4	1923	The Phantom Finn
Glenn Cunningham US	4:6.8	1934	The Iron Horse of Kansas
Gundar Haegg Sweden	4:1.4	1945	Gundar the Wonder
Peter Snell New Zealand	3:54.1	1964	The Man in Black
Jim Ryun US	3:51.1	1967	The Stork In Shorts

— HOLE IN ONE —

The earliest recorded hole in one was achieved by Young Tom Morris in the 1868 Open championship at Prestwick, Scotland, on the eighth hole.

— PARTICIPATION AT SUMMER OLYMPIC GAMES —

	Year	Venue	Nations	Women	Men	Total
I	1896	Athens, Greece	13	-	311	311
II	1900	Paris, France	22	11	1,319	1,330
III	1904	St Louis, USA	12	6	681	687
*	1906	Athens, Greece	20	7	877	884
IV	1908	London, England	23	36	1,999	2,035
V	1912	Stockholm, Sweden	28	57	2,490	2,547
VI	1916	Berlin, Germany	Not held due to First World War			
VII	1920	Antwerp, Belgium	29	64	2,543	2,607
VIII	1924	Paris, France	44	136	2,956	3,092
IX	1928	Amsterdam, Netherlands	46	290	2,724	3,014
X	1932	Los Angeles, USA	37	127	1,281	1,408
XI	1936	Berlin, Germany	49	328	3,738	4,066
XII	1940	Tokyo, then Helsinki	Not held due to Second World War			
XIII	1944	London, England	Not held due to Second World War			

PARTICIPATION AT
— SUMMER OLYMPIC GAMES (CONT'D) —

XIV	1948	London, England	59	385	3,714	4,099
XV	1952	Helsinki, Finland	69	518	4,407	4,925
XVI	1956	Melbourne, Australia	67	384	2,958	3,342
XVII	1960	Rome, Italy	83	610	4,738	5,348
XVIII	1964	Tokyo, Japan	93	683	4,457	5,140
XIX	1968	Mexico City, Mexico	112	781	4,750	5,531
XX	1972	Munich, FRG	122	1,299	5,848	7,147
XXI	1976	Montreal, Canada	92	1,251	4,834	6,085
XXII	1980	Moscow, USSR	81	1,088	4,265	5,353
XXIII	1984	Los Angeles, USA	141	1,620	5,458	7,078
XXIV	1988	Seoul, Korea	159	2,438	6,983	9,421
XXV	1992	Barcelona, Spain	173	2,851	7,108	9,959
XXVI	1996	Atlanta, USA	197	3,523	6,797	10,320
XXVII	2000	Sydney, Australia	199	4,069	6,582	10,651

This celebration, held to mark the tenth anniversary of the modern Games, is not recognised as official by the IOC because it fell outside the agreed four-year cycle for the Games. But results from it are routinely included in books of Olympic records.

— OLDEST WORLD TITLE —

Probably awarded in real tennis, where the first world champion was the Frenchman Clergé, in 1740. His first name is not recorded.

THE MANCHESTER UNITED
FOOTBALLERS WHO LOST THEIR LIVES IN
— THE MUNICH AIR DISASTER OF FEBRUARY 1958 —

Geoff Bent, aged 25
Roger Byrne (captain), aged 29
Eddie Colman, aged 21
Duncan Edwards, aged 21
Mark Jones, aged 24
David Pegg, aged 22
Tommy Taylor, aged 26
Liam Whelan, aged 22

Nine players survived, of whom two, Johnny Berry and Jackie Blanchflower, would not play again.

— OLYMPIC DEMONSTRATION SPORTS —

Since 1904 demonstration sports have been held at the Olympics but not as official events eligible for medals. Initially they provided a showcase for sports unique to the host country, but have since become an important way for a sport to seek full Olympic event status. While basketball, badminton, baseball, curling, freestyle skiing, short-track speed skating, Taekwondo and tennis have all progressed in this way, other sports made only one appearance as demonstration sports:

American Football: 1932 Los Angeles
Australian Rules Football: 1956 Melbourne
Bandy: 1952 Winter Games, Oslo, Norway
Budo (Japanese archery/wrestling/fencing): 1964, Tokyo
Dog Sled Racing: 1932, Lake Placid
Field Handball: 1952, Helsinki
Gliding: 1936, Berlin
Korfball: 1928, Amsterdam
Kayaking and Canadian Canoeing: 1924, Paris
Roller Hockey: 1992, Barcelona
Water Skiing: 1972, Munich
Winter Pentathlon (Cross-country and downhill
skiing/pistol/fencing/horse riding): 1948, St Moritz, Switzerland

— *THE MARQUESS OF QUEENSBERRY RULES* —

The code of rules governing boxing were written by John Graham Chambers, a Cambridge University athlete. First published in 1867, the rules were sponsored by Sir John Sholto Douglas, ninth Marquess of Queensberry and superseded an earlier code written in 1743 by Jack Broughton, a well-known British boxer, which was known as the *London Prize Ring Rules*. The Queensberry Rules were first used in 1972 at a professional tournament in London. They have been adopted worldwide since, with only minor changes.

Rule 1 – To be a fair stand-up boxing match in a 24-foot ring, or as near that size as practicable.

— *THE MARQUESS OF QUEENSBERRY RULES* (CONT'D) —

Rule 2 – No wrestling or hugging allowed.

Rule 3 – The rounds are to be of three minutes' duration, and one minute's time between rounds.

Rule 4 – If either man falls through weakness or otherwise, he must get up unassisted, ten seconds to be allowed for him to do so, the other man meanwhile to return to his corner, and when the fallen man is on his legs the round is to be resumed and continued until the three minutes have expired. If one man fails to come to the scratch in the ten seconds allowed, it shall be in the power of the referee to give his award in favour of the other man.

Rule 5 – A man hanging on the ropes in a helpless state, with his toes off the ground, shall be considered down.

Rule 6 – No seconds or any other person to be allowed in the ring during the rounds.

Rule 7 – Should the contest be stopped by any unavoidable interference, the referee to name the time and place as soon as possible for finishing the contest; so that the match must be won and lost, unless the backers of both men agree to draw the stakes.

Rule 8 – The gloves to be fair-sized boxing gloves of the best quality and new.

Rule 9 – Should a glove burst, or come off, it must be replaced to the referee's satisfaction.

Rule 10 – A man on one knee is considered down and if struck is entitled to the stakes.

Rule 11 – No shoes or boots with springs are allowed.

Rule 12 – The contest in all other respects to be governed by revised rules of the *London Prize Ring*.

— GOLF ON THE MOON —

In February 1971 Captain Alan Shepard, Commander of the Apollo 14 spacecraft, hit two golf balls on the moon with a Spalding six-iron, which he presented in 1974 to the US Golf Association museum in Far Hills, New Jersey. One ball, according to Shepard, 'went for miles and miles'.

— THE RUINOUS GAME OF CROQUET —

The Victorians may have believed sport was healthy and character-building for men, but conservative elements within 19th-century society were convinced that the growing popularity of activities such as cycling and croquet represented a danger to women. An article published in the *American Christian Review* in 1878 described a woman's downfall in 12 steps:

1. A social party
2. Social and play party
3. Croquet party
4. Picnic and croquet party
5. Picnic, croquet and dance
6. Absence from church
7. Imprudent or immoral conduct
8. Exclusion from church
9. A runaway match
10. Poverty and discontent
11. Shame and disgrace
12. Ruin

— ODDJOB FOR OLYMPIC MEDAL WINNER —

American weightlifter Harold Sakata won a silver medal in the light heavyweight division at the 1948 Games in London, England. After a stint as a professional wrestler, he found lasting fame as Oddjob, the bowler-hatted baddie in the 1964 James Bond film, *Goldfinger*.

— HOLARI —

This Turkish variant of hockey takes its name from the wooden wedge or cylinder used in place of a ball. Sticks are wooden, there are no rules, no restrictions on player numbers, but the objective, to score goals, is the same as in conventional hockey. There are no set times, so games sometimes start at daybreak and end at nightfall.

— BASEBALL POSITIONS —

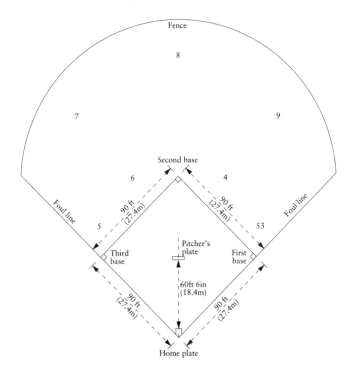

SPORTSMEN WHO HAVE RECEIVED
— THE PRESIDENTIAL MEDAL OF FREEDOM —

The Presidential Medal of Freedom is America's highest civilian award, ranking second only to the Congressional Medal of Honour, the nation's highest military award. Recipients have ranged from politicians such as former German chancellor Helmut Kohl to movie stars such as James Cagney. So far ten sportsmen have received the Presidential Medal of Freedom:

1963	Bob Kiphuth (Yale and US Olympic swimming coach) *presented by John F Kennedy*
1976	Jesse Owens (athletics) *presented by Gerald Ford*
1977	Joe DiMaggio (baseball) *presented by Gerald Ford*
1983	Paul 'Bear' Bryant (University of Alabama football coach) *presented by Ronald Reagan*
1986	Jackie Robinson (baseball) *presented by Ronald Reagan*
1986	Earl 'Red' Blaik (Army football coach) *presented by Ronald Reagan*
1991	Ted Williams (baseball) *presented by George Bush*
1992	Richard Petty (NASCAR motor racing) *presented by George Bush*
1993	Arthur Ashe, Jr (tennis professional) *presented by Bill Clinton*
2002	Hank Aaron (baseball player) *presented by George W Bush*

Bryant and Ashe were honoured posthumously for their achievements.

— SOME INFORMATION ABOUT ROAD BOWLING —

Road Bowling is played generally with a 28oz (0.79kg) cast iron bowl, about 2¼in (57mm) in diameter, on selected public roads. All that is required is appropriate clothing, a bowl and a suitable road. The objective is to cover the course in the least number of shots.

Until the end of the 19th century, the game was not played over a particular distance; instead the winner was decided by who could throw the furthest over 20 shots. The term score represented 20 (*scor*, an Irish word meaning 20) and thus a match is still referred to as a score. Two, three or four players or teams can compete in any one score.

Current strongholds of bowling are Armagh and parts of Tyrone in Ulster; Cork, Waterford and parts of Limerick in Munster; and Mayo in Connacht.

Governing body: Bol Chumann Na Heireann.

Particular attention should be paid to the following rules:

Do not throw the bowl until the referee allows you to do so. Safety and consideration for other road users should be of paramount importance.

The distance covered by the bowl is marked by a scud of grass.

— FASTEST BOOKING IN ENGLISH SOCCER —

Hollywood hardman Vinnie Jones was booked after just three seconds – before the ball had actually left the centre circle – in Chelsea's FA Cup 5th round tie against Sheffield United on 15 February 1992, beating his own record of five seconds when playing for Sheffield United at Manchester City on 19 January 1991.

— ROGER BANNISTER'S FOUR-MINUTE MILE... —

...was set in a blustery wind on the cinder track at Iffley Road, Oxford on 6 May 1954, starting at 6:08pm, in a match race between Oxford University and the Amateur Athletic Association. Bannister had the help of two pacemakers and the splits were as follows.

Chris Brasher	quarter mile	57.5sec
Chris Brasher	half mile	1min 58sec
Chris Chataway	three-quarter mile	3min 0.4sec
Roger Bannister	mile	3min 59.4sec

— RAFT RACE —

The longest raft race in Europe is considered to be the 100-mile (160km) event down the river Wye, in Great Britain, from Hay on Wye to Chepstow, held since 1978, and for which the record time is 10 hours, 19 minutes, nine seconds.

— UNDER ORDERS —

On the eve of their 1938 World Cup final against Hungary, each member of the Italy squad received a three-word telegram from Mussolini. It read: 'Win or die.' Luckily for them, the Italians won 4–2.

— ATHLETES ON *SGT PEPPER* COVER —

The three athletes on the cover of The Beatles' *Sergeant Pepper's Lonely Hearts Club Band* are:

> Johnny Weissmüller, (born 2 June 1904, died 20 January 1984). As a swimmer he won three gold medals at the 1924 Olympics (100m freestyle, 400m freestyle and 100m freestyle relay) and two more (100m freestyle and 100m freestyle relay) at the 1928 Games. Weissmüller then went on to become Hollywood's most famous Tarzan.

> Albert Stubbins, (born 13 July 1919, died 29 December 2002). A footballer who made his professional debut with Newcastle United, but went on to greater glory as a

— ATHLETES ON *SGT PEPPER* COVER (CONT'D) —

centre-forward for Liverpool, making 180 appearances and scoring 83 goals for the club between 1946 and 1952. The team won the League title in the 1946–47 season.

Sonny Liston, (born 8 May 1922, died 30 December 1970). Heavyweight boxing champion from 1962–64, who knocked out Floyd Patterson in the first round to take the title and then did it again to defend it. But Sonny's reign was short-lived as he lost the title to Cassius Clay (Muhammad Ali) in 1964. Fight record of 50–4 with 39 KOs.

— SHOULDERS —

Cornell came up with a novel technique for blocking a Princeton field goal attempt when the two colleges' American football squads met on 9 October 1965. As Princeton kicker Charlie Gogolak prepared to take the kick, Cornell defensive backs Jim Docherty and Dale Witwer climbed on to the shoulders of tackles Reeve Vanneman and Harry Garman to form human towers. Unfortunately for the defence, they were penalised five yards for offside, giving Princeton a first down that eventually led to a touchdown. Cornell tried the trick twice more in the game, but it failed to stop Gogolak kicking both field goals over the heads of his high-rise opponents. Princeton won the game 36–27. Later that year, the human tower was declared illegal by the sport's rules committee.

— THE GOOGLY —

Cricket delivery in which an off-break is bowled to a right-handed batsman with an action that makes it look as if it will break to leg. The inventor was one BJT Bosanquet, who used the delivery against the Australians in 1903. It is known as 'a bosey' in Australia.

LITTLE-KNOWN FACTS
— ABOUT STANLEY MATTHEWS —

- The footballing legend's father, Jack, was a professional boxer known as 'the Fighting Barber'.

- His only hat-trick for England was in a 1937 game against Czechoslovakia, which England won 5–4.

- In 1955, he was the first person chosen to appear on the television show *This Is Your Life*.

- Although he was 45 years old when he rejoined Stoke City in October 1961, attendance at home games jumped from 9,000 to 35,000.

- In 1965 he became the first footballer to receive a knighthood.

— SKELETON —

Skeleton is a variant of cresta, which involves lying flat on a sled. Named as such because originally the shape of the sled used was similar to a skeleton (as opposed to the 'feet-down' style of bob), the sledder lies with head down the slope, usually a bobsled or luge track of about 1,500m (1,640yds). Skeleton became an Olympic sport in 2002. The sled is made of steel or fibreglass and is no more than 120cm (4ft) long. Sledders wear downhill skiing style helmets, shoes with spikes like those of 100m sprinters for the running start and put padding under their catsuits to ease out the bumps. Speeds can reach 130kph (80mph), with up to 4G in the corners. Having hot runners is an advantage, so runner temperature is closely monitored, and has to be within 4°C (39°F) of that of the runners of a reference sled. The temperatures of the reference sled, air and ice are shown on a board at the event for competitors to refer to.

— VINCE LOMBARDI QUOTES —

Vince Lombardi (1913–70) was the greatest American football coach of all time, transforming the Green Bay Packers from a losing side to a team that won five NFL titles and enjoyed victories in the first two Super Bowls (1967 and 1968).

'Dancing is a contact sport. Football is a hitting sport.'

'Football is a game that requires the constant conjuring of animosity.'

'Teams do not go physically flat, they go mentally stale.'

'Success demands singleness of purpose.'

'People who work together will win, whether it be against complex football defences or the problems of modern society.'

'Some of us will do our jobs well and some will not, but we will be judged by only one thing – the result.'

'The good Lord gave you a body that can stand most anything. It's your mind you have to convince.'

'Once you learn to quit, it becomes a habit.'

'It's not whether you get knocked down, it's whether you get up.'

'They may not love you at the time, but they will later.'

'If you aren't fired with enthusiasm, you'll be fired with enthusiasm.'

'Winning isn't everything; it's the only thing.'

'A dictionary is the only place that success comes before work.'

'If it doesn't matter who wins or loses, then why do they keep score?'

'Practice does not make perfect. Only perfect practice makes perfect.'

'Show me a good loser, and I'll show you a loser.'

'Some people try to find things in this game that don't exist but football is only two things – blocking and tackling.'

'Winners never quit and quitters never win.'

'Winning is a habit. Unfortunately, so is losing.'

'The Green Bay Packers never lost a football game. They just ran out of time.'

— SPOCK ROWS TO GOLD —

Benjamin Spock, who went on to make a fortune as author of the best-selling *Common Sense Book Of Baby And Child Care*, won a gold medal for rowing at the 1924 Olympics in Paris, France.

BROTHERS WHO HAVE
— PLAYED IN SOCCER WORLD CUPS —

1930	Mario and Juan Evaristo (Argentina)
1954	Fritz and Otmar Walter (West Germany)
1966	Jack and Bobby Charlton (England)
1974/1978	René and Willy van der Kerkhoff (Netherlands)
1982	Karl-Heinz and Bernd Förster (West Germany)
1990	Ibrahim and Hossam Hassan (Egypt)
1994/98	Frank and Ronald De Boer (Netherlands)
2002	Michal and Marcin Zewlakov (Poland)

— SILVER FOR THE WINNER —

Winners at the first two Olympics of the modern era did not receive gold medals. Instead they were rewarded with a silver medal, a diploma and a crown of olive leaves. Runners-up received a bronze medal and a crown of laurel. Gold medals were introduced at the 1904 St Louis Olympics.

— BOXER PROTESTS WITH RING SIT-IN —

At the 1988 Seoul Olympics Korean bantamweight boxer Byun Jong-il lost his bout with Alexander Hristov of Bulgaria after being penalised for head butting. Objecting to the decision, Jong-il staged a sit-down protest in the ring that lasted one hour and seven minutes.

MOST APPEARANCES IN
— RYDER CUP FOR USA AND EUROPE —

Nick Faldo (GB)	11	1977–97
Christy O'Conner Snr (GB)	10	1955–73
Bernhard Langer (Ger)	10	1981–2002
Dai Rees (GB)	9	1937–61
Billy Casper (US)	8	1961–75
Ray Floyd (US)	8	1969–93
Lanny Watkins (US)	8	1977–93

— RECORD SIGNING —

Signed on 9 February 1979, the transfer of
Trevor Francis from Birmingham City to
Nottingham Forest was the first £1 million
($1.6 million) deal in British football.

— *SPORTS ILLUSTRATED*'S MOST CROWDED COVER —

For its look back on the past year in sport, the 8
February 1984 issue (Volume 60, Issue 6) of the
American magazine featured the following
athletes on its cover.

Dale Murphy, Baseball, Atlanta Braves
Rod Carew, Baseball, California Angels
Steve Carlton, Baseball, Philadelphia Phillies
Kareem Abdul-Jabbar, Basketball, Los Angeles Lakers
Terry Cummings, Basketball, San Diego Clippers
Sam Bowie, Basketball, Kentucky Wildcats
Thurl Bailey, Basketball, North Carolina State Wolfpack
Sidney Lowe, Basketball, North Carolina State Wolfpack
Dereck Whittenburg, Basketball, North Carolina State Wolfpack
Roberto Duran, Boxing
Marvin Hagler, Boxing
Larry Holmes, Boxing
Mike Rozier, American Football, University of Nebraska Cornhuskers
Eric Dickerson, American Football, Los Angeles Rams
Andra Franklin, American Football, Miami Dolphins
Dan Marino, American Football, Miami Dolphins

John Riggins, American Football, Washington Redskins
Herschel Walker, American Football, New Jersey Generals
Tom Watson, Golf
Bill Smith, Hockey, New York Islanders
Sunny's Halo, Horseracing
John McEnroe, Tennis
Martina Navratilova, Tennis
Carl Lewis, Track and Field
Edwin Moses, Track and Field

Model Cheryl Tiegs and sportscaster Howard Cosell were in there too.

— FAST LEARNERS CLINCH BOBSLED GOLD —

The four-man team that represented the USA in the bobsled competition at the 1928 Winter Games in St Moritz ranks as one of the most ad hoc squads ever assembled. The driver was a 16-year-old, Billy Fiske, and the other team members, Nion Tucker, Geoffrey Mason and Richard Parke, were recruited through a small ad placed in the Paris edition of a New York newspaper. When they began practice 18 days before the event, none of the three newcomers had ever been in a bobsled before. They went on to win gold all the same.

— MUHAMMAD ALI QUOTES —

'A man who views the world the same at 50 as he did at 20 has wasted 30 years of his life.'

'Boxing is a lot of white men watching two black men beat each other up.'

'Champions aren't made in gyms. Champions are made from something they have deep inside them – a desire, a dream, a vision. They have to have last-minute stamina, they have to be a little faster, they have to have the skill and the will. But the will must be stronger than the skill.'

'I am America. I am the part you won't recognise. But get used to me. Black, confident, cocky; my name, not yours; my religion, not yours; my goals, my own; get used to me.'

— MUHAMMAD ALI QUOTES (CONT'D) —

'I got nothing against no Viet Cong. No Vietnamese ever called me a nigger.'

'I know I got it made while the masses of black people are catchin' hell, but as long as they ain't free, I ain't free.'

'I'm not the greatest; I'm the double greatest. Not only do I knock 'em out, I pick the round.'

'It's just a job. Grass grows, birds fly, waves pound the sand. I beat people up.'

'Life is a gamble. You can get hurt, but people die in plane crashes, lose their arms and legs in car accidents; people die every day. Same with fighters: some die, some get hurt, some go on. You just don't let yourself believe it will happen to you.'

'Only a man who knows what it is like to be defeated can reach down to the bottom of his soul and come up with the extra ounce of power it takes to win when the match is even.'

'Only the nose knows where the nose goes when the doors close.'

'Service to others is the rent you pay for your room here on earth.'

'Superman don't need no seatbelt.'

'The man who has no imagination has no wings.'

'There are more pleasant things to do than beat up people.'

'When you can whip any man in the world, you never know peace.'

'Float like a butterfly, sting like a bee, your hands can't hit what your eyes can't see.'

'The fight is won or lost far away from witnesses – behind the lines, in the gym, and out there on the road, long before I dance under those lights.'

'I'm so fast that last night I turned off the light switch in my hotel room and was in bed before the room was dark.'

'That all you got George?' (Into Foreman's ear during a clinch late in the Rumble In The Jungle in Zaire on 30 October 1974.)

'Be loud, be pretty and keep their black-hating asses in their chairs.'

— BULLY OFF —

To get a hockey match under way, one player from each side stands facing the other with the ball between them on the ground. They alternately tap their sticks together and hit the ground, three times for each, before going for the ball.

— MOST WINS IN HEAVYWEIGHT TITLE FIGHTS —

Fighter	Bouts	Wins
Joe Louis	27	26
Muhammad Ali	25	22
Larry Holmes	25	21
Lennox Lewis	15	14
Tommy Burns	13	12
Mike Tyson	15	12

— 'THE CHEATING SWORDSMAN' —

Boris Onishchenko was given this nickname after his attempt to cheat in the fencing section of the modern pentathlon at the Montreal Olympics in 1976. His épée (sword) had been wired up to trigger the electronic scoring system and register hits as and when he wanted. Onishchenko, an army officer from the Ukraine who had won silver in Munich in 1972 was duly disqualified after complaints from the British team led to the weapon being examined by judges.

— SUMO RANKINGS —

Sumo rankings are based on winning a series of fights. The wrestlers, called either *sumotori* or more informally *rikishi* are ranked in an official list, the *banzuke*, published by the sport's governing body, the Nihon Sumo Kyokui. They can drop down a ranking if they lose, apart from those of the highest rank, the *yokozuna*, who tend to retire if they don't perform.

— SUMO RANKINGS (CONT'D) —

The top five ranks from yokozuna to *maegashira* are called *maku uchi*, and the ranking runs in this order:

yokozuna*
ozeki
sekiwake
komusubi
maegashira
juryo**
makushita
sandamme
jonidan
jonokuchi

(highest rank, title created in the 17th century, only attained by 67 sumotori)

**(sumotori at this level and above wear ceremonial aprons known as* kesho mawashi, *which are made of silk and studded with gold, silver or diamonds)*

— THE CURSE OF IBROX —

With three fatal crowd disasters in 70 years, Ibrox Park in Glasgow, home of Rangers, would be a leading contender for the unluckiest stadium in soccer. The curse started in April 1902, when part of the West Stand collapsed during a Scotland v England international; 23 died, and 364 were injured. The result, a 1–1 draw, was scratched from international records. In September 1961 a stand pillar collapsed, and three fans died, while in January 1971 fans crushed down a stairway during an 'Old Firm' derby between Rangers and Celtic and 66 died.

— THE 'HARVEY SMITH' —

The term dates back to 1971 when the showjumper of that name was competing in the prestigious Hickstead Derby. Smith had won the previous year but forgot to bring the trophy with him and received an earbashing from vice president Douglas Bunn. Smith duly completed his victorious clear round and stuck up two fingers at the judges as he left the arena. He was promptly disqualified for what judges considered 'a disgusting gesture'. Smith claimed, 'It was a V for victory. Churchill used it throughout the war.' He was reinstated after showing the stewards photos of Churchill making the gesture, which has been known as a 'Harvey Smith' ever since.

— ERIC CANTONA QUOTES —

The arrival of France international soccer player Eric Cantona at Manchester United in November 1992 galvanised the side. In the next five years until his retirement in 1997, United won the league four times and the FA Cup twice, assuring the striker a lasting place in the hearts of fans. On the pitch, he played with passion and flair and was no stranger to controversy. Off it, his eloquence and penchant for philosophising marked him as one of the game's most unique characters.

'When the seagulls follow the trawler, it is because they think sardines will be thrown into the sea.'

'An artist, in my eyes, is someone who can lighten up a dark room. I have never, and will never, find any difference between the pass from Pelé to Carlos Alberto in the final of the World Cup '70 and the poetry of the young Rimbaud.'

'I'd be an eagle because I love its way of flying and if I were an angel I'd simply be Eric Cantona with big wings.'

'If I were a sport I'd be football, of course, and if I were a film I'd be *Raging Bull*.'

'If I were any child I would be my children but if I were Eric Cantona I'd be proud.'

'I have inherited my father's capacity to completely vanish in a second, to be elsewhere.'

'I play with passion and fire. I have to accept that sometimes this fire does. harm. I cannot be what I am without these sides to my character.'

— OLYMPIC CLOTHING AND DRESS —

General Clothing
The following items of clothing are being supplied

Men
1 blazer; 1 pair slacks; 1 shirt; 1 tie; 1 pair shoes.

Women
1 skirt and jacket; 1 blouse; 1 pair shoes; bra.

All Team Members
1 tracksuit; 1 towelling top; 1 sports shirt; socks.

Dress for Travel
The group will wear the following uniform (issued by BOA) in transit to the Games:

Men	Women
Blazer	Blazer
Trousers	Skirt
Shirt	Blouse
Tie	Shoes
Shoes	

Personal
All staying in the Village must bring their own soap and towels, and the men their own shoe-cleaning materials. None will be available in the Olympic village.

From the official handbook of Great Britain's Olympic team, 22nd Summer Olympic Games in Moscow, 1980.

— MARATHON STANDARDISED —

The length of the marathon was not standardised in the Olympics until 1924, when it was decided to adopt the same length as was used in 1908: 26 miles and 385yds (42.186km). The other distances used were:

1896 and 1904: 40km
1900: 40.26km
1906: 41.86km
1912: 40.2km
1920: 42.75km

— GOLF-FINGER —

The golf match in the James Bond film *Goldfinger* (1962) was filmed at Stoke Poges golf club in Buckinghamshire, close to Pinewood studios. Both the writer Ian Fleming and the film's Bond, Sean Connery, were keen golfers, Fleming being a member of Royal St George's, Sandwich, and Connery a member of the Royal & Ancient.

— HIGHEST EARNING SPORTS FILMS —

Film, Date (sport)

Male lead	Female lead	Director	Takings (US$)
Rocky IV, 1985 (Boxing)			
Sylvester Stallone	Brigitte Neilsen	Stallone	300,500,000
Jerry Maguire, 1996 (American football)			
Tom Cruise	Renee Zellweger	Cameron Crowe	273,600,000
Space Jam, 1996 (Basketball)			
Bill Murray & Michael Jordan	n/a	Joe Pytha	225,400,000
The Waterboy, 1998 (American football)			
Adam Sandler	Kathy Bates	Frank Coraci	190,200,000
Days Of Thunder, 1990 (Stock car racing)			
Cruise	Nicole Kidman	Tony Scott	165,900,000
Cool Runnings, 1993 (Bobsleighing)			
Leon	n/a	Jon Turteltaub	154,900,000
A League Of Their Own, 1992 (Baseball)			
Tom Hanks	Geena Davis	Penny Marshall	130,500,000
Remember The Titans, 2000 (American football)			
Denzel Washington	n/a	Boaz Yakin	130,000,000
Rocky III, 1982 (Boxing)			
Stallone	Talia Shire	Stallone	122,800,000
Rocky V, 1990 (Boxing)			
Stallone	Shire	John Avildsen	120,000,000

— FREESTYLE RECORD BREAKER —

On 18 July 1905, J Scott Leary of the Olympic Club, San Francisco, became the first man to swim the 100yds freestyle in one minute.

— FLAMING BOAT —

At the 1976 Montreal Olympics, British yachtsmen David Hunt and Alan Warren hoped to improve on the silver medal they won in the Tempest sailing class at the Munich Games four years earlier. When they failed to win a medal of any colour, they vented their frustration by setting fire to their boat.

— MARATHON GRAPPLE —

At the 1912 Stockholm Olympics, a Graeco-Roman wrestling match between Martin Klein of Russia and Alfred Askainen of Finland continued for a gruelling 11 hours before Klein managed to pin his opponent. The Russian was too exhausted by the experience to compete in the final, however, so Claes Johanson of Sweden was awarded the gold medal by default.

— DRAG RACING 'CHRISTMAS TREE' —

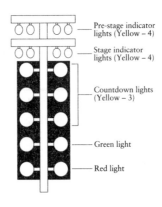

Pre-stage indicator lights (Yellow – 4)

Stage indicator lights (Yellow – 4)

Countdown lights (Yellow – 3)

Green light

Red light

TWENTY-ONE STARS AND
— THE SOCCER CLUBS THEY SUPPORT —

Disgraced British politician and author Jeffrey Archer (Bristol Rovers)
Film director Sir Richard Attenborough (Chelsea)
British prime minister Tony Blair (Newcastle United)
Former Talking Head David Byrne (Dumbarton)
Guitarist Eric Clapton (West Bromwich Albion)
Snooker player Steve Davis (Charlton Athletic)
Tennis player Stefan Edberg (Leeds United)
Governor of the Bank of England Sir Edward George (Manchester City)
Revolutionary icon Che Guevara (Rosario Central, Argentina)
Actor Tom Hanks (Aston Villa)
Film director Spike Lee (Arsenal)
Former Beatle Sir Paul McCartney (Everton)
Comedian Mike Myers (Liverpool)
Formula One racing drivers Ralf and Michael Schumacher (FC Köln)
Film star Omar Sharif (Juventus)
Former MI5 spy David Shayler (Middlesbrough)
Singer Rod Stewart (Celtic)
Singer Shania Twain (Tottenham Hotspur)
Actor Ray Winstone (West Ham United)
Film star Kate Winslet (Reading)
Film star Catherine Zeta Jones (Swansea)

— A SELECTION OF SURF SLANG —

Ankle Busters: Small waves.

Barrel: The hollow channel inside a good wave when it breaks and curls over.

Bone Yard: The area where the waves break.

Coffin: Riding a surfboard while lying stiffly on your back with arms crossed.

Cruncher: A big, hard-breaking wave that folds over and is almost impossible to ride.

Face: The unbroken, nearly vertical front of a wave.

Glasshouse: The space inside a tube (also 'Green Room').

— A SELECTION OF SURF SLANG (CONT'D) —

Goofy-Foot: Riding a surfboard right foot forward (left foot forward is the more common position).

Hang Five/Ten: To place five (or ten) toes over the nose of the board.

Locked In: Firmly set in the curling portion of the wave with water holding down the tail of the board.

Meatball: The yellow flag with the black circle indicating 'No Surfing'.

Over the Falls: To get dragged over as the wave breaks.

Pearl: Driving the nose of a surfboard under water to stop or slow down the ride.

Sand Facial: The result of wiping out and being dragged along the bottom, face first.

Shoot the Curl (or Tube): Riding a surfboard through, or in and out of, the hollow part of the wave formed as it crests over.

Skeg: The fin at the tail end of a surfboard.

Soup: The foam from a broken wave.

Spinner: A surfer making a complete 360-degree turn in an upright position while the surfboard keeps going straight (also called a '360').

Tube: The hollow portion of a wave formed when the crest spills over and makes a tunnel or hollow space in front of the face of the wave.

Walking the Nose: Moving forward on the board toward the front.

— THE IMPREGNABLE QUADRILATERAL —

Name given to victories in the Open and Amateur golf championships of Britain and America, a unique feat achieved by Bobby Jones in the summer of 1930, after which he retired. Jones took the British Amateur between 26 and 31 May at St Andrews (of which he later said, 'I could take out of my life everything except my experiences at St Andrews and still have a rich, full life.'); the British Open at Hoylake, Wirral, between 18 and 20 June; the US Open at Interlachen, Minneapolis between 10 and 12 July; and the US Amateur at Merion between 24 and 27 September. Jones retired soon afterwards to concentrate on his law practice in Atlanta, and founded the Augusta National course and the Masters tournament.

— THE POOLS PANEL —

First convened on 26 January 1963, during one of the hardest winters ever experienced in Britain, when there was massive disruption to football fixtures and postal deliveries, and hence to the football pools industry. The pools is a British soccer-based competition in which, each week, members of the public bet by forecasting games that will end in a tie in which both sides score goals. So badly was the industry hit that Littlewoods made over 800 staff redundant at the end of the winter of 1963. The 'Big Freeze' had begun in mid-December and after five weekends of pools coupons being declared void, a group of experts convened in a London hotel to decide the outcome of postponed matches. The first panel was chaired by Lord Brabazon of Tara and was made up of soccer legends Tom Finney, Ted Drake, Tommy Lawton and George Young, plus a former referee, Arthur Ellis. However expert subsequent panellists were, their success rate at predicting score draws on the five times they met in 1981–82 was zero.

Most celebrated among all Pools Panel tales is the story of the player who heard the Panel had given his side a home win and asked his manager for the win bonus. The manager answered that he had been dropped for the match.

— THE MACPHERSON SHIELD —

Australian entrepreneur Sir MacPherson Robertson (1860–1945) made a fortune from the confectionery empire he founded. After the First World War he enlisted veteran servicemen as salesmen for his company and encouraged them to play croquet, which he believed offered a good training in the skills needed for business success. In 1925, he donated the shield that carries his company name for a croquet competition between Australia and England. In 1930 New Zealand was admitted and the competition became a triangular one. The USA was admitted in 1993 and the tournament is now held every three or four years.

Venue (Year)	Winners	Second	Third	Fourth
NZ (2000)	GB	NZ	USA	Australia
GB (1996)	GB	NZ	Australia	USA
Australia (1993)	GB	NZ	Australia	USA
NZ (1990)	GB	NZ	Australia	
GB (1986)	NZ	GB	Australia	
Australia (1982)	GB	Australia	NZ	
NZ (1979)	NZ	GB	Australia	
England (1974)	GB	NZ	Australia	
Australia (1969)	England	NZ	Australia	
NZ (1963)	England	Australia	NZ	
England (1956)	England	NZ		
NZ (1950–51)	NZ	England		
England (1937)	England	Australia		
Australia (1935)	Australia	England	NZ	
Australia (1930)	Australia	NZ		
Australia (1927–28)	Australia	England		
England (1925)	England	Australia		

— THE SPITZ BLITZ —

This happened in the 1972 Munich Olympics when, over a period of eight days, American swimmer Mark Spitz won all seven events he had entered, setting world records in each one – a feat which has never been surpassed.

Date	Event	Time
28 Aug	200m butterfly	2min 0.7sec
Runner-up: Gary Hall (US)		
28 Aug	4x100m freestyle relay	3min 26.42sec
Runner-up: USSR		
29 Aug	200m freestyle	1min 52.78sec
Runner-up: Steve Genter (US)		
31 Aug	100m butterfly	54.27sec
Runner-up: Bruce Robertson (CAN)		
31 Aug	4x200m freestyle relay	7min 35.78sec
Runner-up: West Germany		
3 Sep	100m freestyle	51.22sec
Runner-up: Jerry Heidenreich (US)		
4 Sep	medley relay*	3min 48.16sec
Runner-up: East Germany		

*Spitz swam the butterfly leg

— TO DIP OR NOT TO DIP? —

US military protocol stipulates that the Stars and Stripes is never dipped, not even to the president. This protocol has been stuck to since the 1936 Berlin Olympics, when the flag was kept upright in front of Adolf Hitler. Before that, however, Old Glory seems to have been dipped and held straight in roughly alternate years. At the 1908 London Games, for example, it was kept upright in front of King Edward VII by a US delegation who were apparently annoyed at the absence of the Stars and Stripes from the flags adorning the stadium.

— ARGYLE —

English soccer team Plymouth Argyle derives its name from the fact that the club was founded in a house in Argyle Terrace in 1886.

— UK FOOTBALL TRANSFER FEE MILESTONES —

1905 First £1,000 transfer – Alf Common from Sunderland to Middlesbrough

1928: First £10,000 transfer – David Jack from Bolton to Arsenal

1961: First £100,000 transfer – Denis Law from Manchester United to Torino

1978: First £500,000 transfer – David Mills from Middlesbrough to West Bromwich Albion

1979 First £1 million transfer – Trevor Francis from Birmingham City to Nottingham Forest

1991 First £5 million transfer – David Platt from Aston Villa to Bari

1999 First £10 million transfer – Chris Sutton from Blackburn Rovers to Chelsea

TOP TEN MEDAL-WINNING — COUNTRIES AT SUMMER OLYMPICS —

	Gold	Silver	Bronze	Total
USA	872	658	586	2116
Russia*	498	409	371	1278
Germany**	214	242	280	736
United Kingdom	180	233	225	638
France	188	193	217	598
Italy	179	143	157	479
Sweden	136	156	177	469
East Germany	159	150	136	445
Hungary	150	135	158	443
Australia	102	110	138	350

includes USSR (1952–88) and Unified team (1992)
** *includes West Germany (1952, 1968–88)*

— UNDERARM BOWLING —

Bowling underarm is permitted in first-class cricket only if it is agreed before the match. It was, however, only removed from the cricket rule book in 2000. The last bowler selected in first class cricket in England specifically as an underarmer is said to have been TJ Moloney of Surrey in 1921.

Underarm was banned in one-day cricket following the infamous Chappell incident of 1 February 1981, when New Zealand needed six runs off the final ball to tie the third final of the Benson & Hedges World Series Cup. Trevor Chappell was ordered by his elder brother Greg, the Australian captain, to bowl the last ball underarm to New Zealand's Brian McKechnie, who blocked the ball and threw his bat away in disgust. Chappell's decision was condemned as 'an act of cowardice' by New Zealand Prime Minister Robert Muldoon.

— SEAMAN'S SAFE HANDS —

Manchester City and former England goalkeeper David Seaman signs his autographs 'Safe Hands'.

— THE BARCLAY MATCH —

Captain Barclay of the Royal Welch Fusiliers walked 1,000 miles (1,609km) in 1,000 hours, 1 mile (1.609km) per hour over 41 days 16 hours, on Newmarket Heath in July 1809. The feat, which became known as the Barclay Match, sparked a number of similar ultra-endurance events during the 19th century. The most notable of these was William Gale's walk of 2,000 miles (3,218km) in 2,000 consecutive hours. Starting on 28 July 1853, Gale took more than 83 days to finish the challenge, making it one of the longest sporting events in history.

— UP A GUM TREE —

A plaque on the 16th hole at Royal Birkdale reading 'Arnold Palmer, the Open Championship 1964' commemorates the place where Palmer found himself in the rough with his ball under a small bush – a virtually unplayable situation. Rather than try to play out onto the fairway, Palmer dug out the ball and bush with his six-iron, sending the ball onto the green, which was 140yds (128m) away, to two-put for par. He went on to win the Open, also winning it the following year as well.

Three years later in the Australian Wills Masters tournament in Melbourne, Palmer again fell foul of foliage when he lifted his second shot at the ninth, 20ft (6m) up into a gum tree. He climbed up and used his number one-iron as a hammer to wallop the ball 30yds (27m) for a simple chip to the green.

— FLOWERS WINS HISTORIC GOLD —

On 19 February 2002, Vonetta Flowers of Birmingham, Alabama, became the first black athlete to win a gold medal at the Winter Olympics after teaming up with driver Jill Bakken to win the inaugural woman's bobsled competition for the USA.

— THE GOLF BALL: A HISTORY —

The first golf ball was the feathery, which consisted of a covering of several layers of tightly-stitched leather stuffed with goose or chicken feathers – a 'gentleman's top hat full' was considered the right amount – that had been boiled to soften them. Once stuffed, the ball was hammered into a sphere and then painted.

Gutta-percha, the evaporated milky juice or gum of a common Malaysian tree, is said to have been used to make golf balls for the first time in 1848 by Rev Dr Robert Adams Paterson. It is a hard and non-brittle substance that becomes soft and malleable when immersed in boiling water, and it was a common packing material in the 19th century. After play, golfers had to boil and roll their balls on a smoothing board to return them to shape.

Golfers discovered that gutta-percha balls flew straighter if a pattern was hammered into the ball's smooth surface. Initially, these patterns aped the stitching of the feathery ball but evolved into the bramble, which had a surface akin to the berry of that name.

The rubber ball was invented in 1898 by an Ohio golfer, Coburn Haskell, and Bertram Work of the BF Goodrich company. It featured a solid rubber core surrounded by wound rubber thread and a gutta-percha cover. Balata, the gum of the bullet or bully tree of South America, replaced gutta-percha as the cover material of choice in the early 1900s. The dimple patterned surface was introduced in 1908.

In 1930 in Britain and 1932 in the USA, golf ball sizes were standardised. Weight was set at a maximum of 1⅔oz (46g) and diameter of 1⅔in (4.26cm).

Modern balls have a covering of either balata, elastomer or Surlyn, a thermoplastic resin. Two types are widely used: a two-piece ball consisting of a cover and a solid core of a rubber compound; and a three-piece ball. The latter has a cover, rubber thread windings and either a solid rubber or elastomer core or a liquid-filled core, a small ball of natural rubber filled with a mixture of water, corn syrup and salt.

— O'REE BECOMES FIRST BLACK PLAYER IN NHL —

Willie O'Ree became the first black player in the NHL when he took to the ice for the Boston Bruins against the Montreal Canadiens on 18 January 1958. The Canadian-born wing's achievement was all the more remarkable for the fact that he had lost the sight in his right eye after being hit by a puck while playing in a junior league game in 1955. O'Rees's career as a Bruin was shortlived, however. He played only two games in the 1957–58 season and a further 41 games in 1960–61, when he scored a modest four goals and ten assists. Traded at the end of the year, he went on to enjoy greater success in the Western Hockey League. He was the league's leading scorer in 1964 and 1969 and was 43 by the time he retired in 1978.

— AIZKOLARIS... —

...is a wood chopping competition held in Spain's Basque country. Most popular is a variant where choppers stand astride logs placed horizontally on the ground and chop them down the middle as quickly as they can. There are usually 6–20 logs, each 3–6ft (91–183cm) thick. Three different kinds of axe, known as an *aizkora* in Basque are used: the *illargi-aizkora* (moon axe), which has a crescent-shaped blade; the *bizkaya aizkora* (Biscay axe) which has a wedge-shaped straight cutting edge sloping back towards the handle; and the *napar aizkora* (Navarre) axe, which has a blade of equal width sloping back towards the handle.

Other *herri kilorak* (Basque 'country sports') include: scything; races in which oxen and donkeys drag stones; running with 200lb (90kg) sacks on the shoulders; throwing hay bales over a rope; and *harrijasotzaile* (stone lifting).

— BASKETBALL'S TOP EARNERS OF 2001–02 —

Kevin Garnett	Minnesota Timberwolves	$22.40m
Shaquille O'Neal	LA Lakers	$21.43m
Alonzo Mourning	Miami Heat	$18.76m
Juwan Howard	Dallas Mavericks	$18.75m
Scottie Pippen	Portland Trailblazers	$18.10m

— REFEREES OF WORLD CUP FINALS —

Year Referee	Venue	Result
1930 Jan Langenus (Belgium)	Montevideo	Uruguay 4 Argentina 2
1934 Ivan Eklind (Sweden)	Rome	Italy 2 Czechoslovakia 1
1938 George Capdeville (France)	Paris	Italy 4 Hungary 2
1950* George Reader (England)	Rio de Janeiro	Uruguay 2 Brazil 1
1954 William Ling (England)	Berne	West Germany 3 Hungary 2
1958 Maurice Guigue (France)	Stockholm	Brazil 5 Sweden 2
1962 Nickolaj Latychev (USSR)	Santiago	Brazil 3 Czechoslovakia 1
1966 Gottfried Dienst (Switzerland)	London	England 4 West Germany 2
1970 Rudolf Gloeckner (GDR)	Mexico City	Brazil 4 Italy 1
1974 John Taylor (England)	Munich	Netherlands 1 West Germany 2
1978 Sergio Gonella (Italy)	Buenos Aires	Argentina 3 Netherlands 1
1982 Arnaldo Coelho (Brazil)	Madrid	Italy 3 West Germany 1
1986 Romualdo Arppi Filho (Brazil)	Mexico City	Argentina 3 West Germany 2
1990 Edgardo Codesal (Mexico)	Rome	West Germany 1 Argentina 0

— REFEREES OF WORLD CUP FINALS (CONT'D) —

1994

Sandor Puhl (Hungary)	Pasadena	Brazil 0 Italy 0 (0–0 aet, Brazil won 3–2 on penalties)
1998		
Said Belqola (Morocco)	Paris	Brazil 0 France 3
2002		
Pierluigi Collina (Italy)	Yokohama	Germany 0 Brazil 2

The 1950 tournament was played on a league basis. By a quirk of the draw Uruguay and Brazil played each other in the last game and finished first and second.

— OLYMPIANS FOR ALL SEASONS —

Only three athletes have won medals at both the winter and summer Olympics.

- Eddie Eagan (USA): light heavyweight boxing gold (Antwerp, 1920) and four-man bobsled gold (Lake Placid, 1932)

- Jacob Tullin Thams (Norway): ski jumping gold (Chamonix, 1924) and eight-metre yachting silver (Berlin, 1936)

- Christa Luding-Rothenburger (East Germany): speed skating 500m gold (Sarajevo, 1984) and 1,000m gold (Calgary, 1988), 500m silver (1988) and 500m bronze (Albertville, 1992) and sprint cycling silver (Seoul, 1988)

— ALBION ON DIPLOMATIC MISSION TO THE ORIENT —

When West Bromwich Albion became the first Western football side to play in China since the Cultural Revolution, the 1978 visit was considered so diplomatically important that Prime Minister Edward Heath met the side to give them a pre-tour pep talk.

— YOGI...UGLIER THAN THE AVERAGE BERRA —

'Sure I'm ugly, but what about it? In this racket, all you have to do is hit the ball and I ain't never seen anybody hit it with his face.' NY Yankee legend Yogi Berra, who incidentally inspired the name of a well-known Hanna-Barbera cartoon character.

— MARATHON EFFORT —

John Stephen Akhwari finished the marathon at the 1968 Olympics more than an hour after winner Mamo Wolde of Ethiopia. Few spectators were left in the stands to witness the bandaged and bloodied Tanzanian's lonely arrival. When asked why he hadn't quit earlier, Akhwari answered, 'My country did not send me to Mexico City to start the race. They sent me here to finish.'

— SOME NOTES ON THE TAILTEANN GAMES —

The Tailteann Games are named after the hill of Tailte, burial mound of Tailtiu, the royal lady of the Fir Bolg. The Games are part of the Irish festival of Lughnasa, a time of feasting, dancing, marriage and displays of skills. Inaugurated in 632 BC, they were held in the first week of August almost without interruption until AD 1169. The Games were revived in 1924 with the gathering of international athletes at Croke Park, Dublin. Today, the modern concept of the Tailteann Games is a festival of school athletics.

Events included:
- A foot race on a chariot course, the winner being the first to finish.

- *Del Chlis* – A spear feat in which the spear is thrown in such a way so as to spin and strike with incredible accuracy. (Something like what rifling in a barrel does for a bullet.)

- Wrestling – A brutal form of unarmed combat. (Not too different from Pancratean, known today as Pankratian.)

- *Roé* – A sword duel using short bladed swords. (Roé is now seen as the Irish marital art of Bata fighting.)

- Running leap over a stream – That's one long jump...

- Tossing of stones – Something like a free-form version of shot put.

— SOME NOTES ON THE TAILTEANN GAMES (CONT'D) —

- Hurley competition
- Spear throw for distance
- Chariot race
- Skill of driving – A chariot team event. The driver must navigate a course of obstacles and the warrior in the back has to grab rings and other items from poles and throw javelins at moving targets.

— WORLD CUP FINAL HEADED GOALS —

Year Final Score	Match Scorer	Team	Scoreline	Minute
1958 Sweden-Brazil				
2–5	Pele	Brazil	2–5	90
1962 Brazil-Czechoslovakia				
3–1	Zito	Brazil	2–1	69
1966 England-West Germany				
4–2 aet	Geoff Hurst	England	1–1	18
1978 Argentina-Netherlands				
3–1 aet	Dick Nanninga	Netherlands	1–1	82
1986 Argentina-West Germany				
3–2	Jose Luis Brown	Argentina	1–0	23
1986 Argentina-West Germany				
3–2	Rudi Voeller	West Germany	2–2	82
1998 Brazil-France				
0–3	Zinadine Zidane	France	0–1	27
1998 Brazil-France				
0–3	Zinadine Zidane	France	0–2	45

— PHOTO-FINISH DEBUTS IN LONDON —

The photo-finish camera was introduced at the 1948 Olympics in London. Judges first used it to determine the result of the 100m final, awarding victory to the USA's Harrison Dillard over his compatriot Barney Ewell.

— FROM ROSEBUDS TO BLACKHAWKS —

The Chicago Blackhawks were originally the
Portland Rosebuds and played in the Pacific
Coast Hockey Association. When that league
folded in 1926, the Rosebuds were bought by
Major Frederic McLaughlin, a Chicago
entrepreneur who had made a fortune in the
coffee business. He owned a restaurant called the
Blackhawk, so named because he commanded the
333rd Machine Gun Battalion of the US Army's
85th (Blackhawk) Division in the First World
War, and decided to give his new team the same
name as a cheap way of advertising the eatery.

— TOO TALL TO SHOOT HOOPS —

In 1936, the International Basketball Federation seriously considered
banning players of 6ft 3in (1.905m) and taller.

— BORN UNDER A RED STAR —

Names of East European sports teams often date back to the
Communist era, when clubs were called after whatever branch of
the state they represented.

Dynamo	State security apparatus	Dynamo Kiev
CSKA	Specifically the Red Army in Russia	CSKA Moscow
Red Star	Army	Red Star Belgrade
Spartak	Worker's collective	Spartak Moscow
Lokomotiv	Railway workers	Lokomotiv Moscow
Metallurg	Metal workers	Metallurg Donetsk
Metallist	Metal workers	Metallist Kharkov

— GOLDEN AGE OF 13 —

Marjorie Gestring is the youngest person to have
won an individual gold medal at the Olympics.
The American diver's victory in the women's
springboard event at the 1936 Games came when
she was 13 years 9 months old.

— THE LONELINESS OF A HOCKEY GOALIE —

'If you make a mistake, they turn on a red light behind you, a siren goes off and thousands of people scream.' Hockey Hall of Fame goaltender Jacques Plante, who led the Montreal Canadiens to six Stanley Cup victories (1953, 1956–60), on the pressures of playing in goal.

— DWARFS AND DODOS REIGN SUPREME —

Cape Coast Dwarfs were football champions of Ghana in 1968, and FC Dodo won the title race in Mauritius in 1970.

— VENUES FOR THE 2006 WORLD CUP —

City	Population	Stadium	Capacity
Berlin	3.4 million	Olympicstadion	76,000
*Frankfurt	650,000	Waldstadion	48,000
Hannover	525,000	Niedersachsenstadion	45,000
*Munich	1.3 million	Stadion Munchen	66,000
Cologne	1 million	Stadion Köln	45,000
*Gelsenkirchen	285,000	Arena Auf Schalke	52,000
Kaiserslautern	100,000	Fritz-Walter-Stadion	48,500
Nuremberg	490,000	Frankenstadion	45,500
Dortmund	400,000	Westfalenstadion	50,000
*Leipzig	530,000	Zentralstadion	42,655
Stuttgart	550,000	Gottlieb-Daimler-Stadion	51,000

denotes new stadium built for the World Cup

— ROY 'WRONG WAY' RIEGELS —

The 1929 Rose Bowl between California Golden Bears and Georgia Tech featured one of the most misguided plays in American football history. California centre Roy Riegels recovered a fumble on the Georgia 36-yard line and took off for the end zone. But in dodging a tackle, he lost his bearings and began heading in the opposite direction. After running the wrong way for 70yds, he was finally stopped when California quarterback Benny Lom grabbed him on his own team's 3-yard line. The blunder cost California a safety and the match, which they lost 8–7, and it provided Riegels with a nickname that would dog him for the rest of his career – Roy 'Wrong Way' Riegels.

— UBALDO WINS...AGAIN —

Gubbio, northern Italy, is the home of a race that has been fixed since the Middle Ages. It is held each May in honour of St Ubaldo, who saved the town from invasion in the 12th century. During the annual Feast of Candles, statues of Saints Ubaldo, George and Anthony are paraded through the town atop 30ft (9.1m) poles and then raced up the nearby 2,690ft (820m) Monte Ingino. The result is never in doubt, though, as by centuries-old tradition the saints and their bearers always finish in the same order: Ubaldo wins, followed by George and Anthony.

MOST SUCCESSFUL TEAMS IN — BASEBALL'S WORLD SERIES 1903–2002 —

Team	League*	Appearances	Wins
New York Yankees	AL	38	26
Philadelphia-Kansas City-Oakland Athletics	AL	14	9
St Louis Cardinals	NL	15	9
Brooklyn-Los Angeles Dodgers	NL	18	6
Boston Red Sox	AL	9	5
Cincinnati Reds	NL	9	5
New York-San Francisco Giants	NL	17	5
Pittsburgh Pirates	NL	7	5
Detroit Tigers	AL	9	4
Baltimore Orioles	AL	7	3
Boston-Milwaukee-Atlanta Braves	NL	9	3
Washington Senators-Minnesota Twins	AL	6	3

MOST SUCCESSFUL TEAMS IN
— BASEBALL'S WORLD SERIES 1903–2002 (CONT'D) —

Chicago Cubs	NL	10	2
Chicago White Sox	AL	4	2
Cleveland Indians	AL	5	2
New York Mets	NL	4	2
Toronto Blue Jays	AL	2	2

*AL = American League. NL = National League.
AL teams have won the series 58 times; NL teams have won it 40 times.

The Athletics played in Philadelphia 1901–54 and Kansas City 1955–67
The Dodgers played in Brooklyn 1890–1957
The Giants played in New York 1883–1957
The Braves played in Boston 1876–1952 and Milwaukee 1953–65
The Senators played in Washington DC 1901–60 then changed their name
    when the franchise moved in 1961.

— THE WORLD OF WINKS —

The English Tiddlywinks Association was founded in 1958 to promote the adult version of the game. As its website (www.etwa.org) notes, winks has a very colourful vocabulary. Here is a glossary of some of the most common terms in use:

Blitz: an attempt to pot all six of your own colour early in the game (generally before many squoops have been taken).

Bomb: to send a wink at a pile, usually from distance, in the hope of significantly disturbing it.

Boondock: to play a squopped wink a long way away, usually while keeping your own wink(s) in the battle area.

Bring-in: an approach shot.

Bristol: a shot that attempts to jump a pile onto another wink; the shot is played by holding the squidger at right angles to its normal plane.

Carnovsky: a successful pot from the baseline (that is, from 3ft [91cm] away).

Crud: a physically hard shot whose purpose is to destroy a pile completely.

Doubleton: a pile in which two winks are covered up by a single enemy wink.

Good Shot: named after John Good. The shot consists of playing a flat wink through a nearby pile in the hope of destroying it.

Gromp: an attempt to jump a pile onto another wink (usually with the squidger held in a conventional rather than Bristol fashion).

John Lennon Memorial Shot: a simultaneous boondock and squop.

Knock-off: to knock the squopping wink off a pile.

Lunch: to pot a squopped wink (usually belonging to an opponent).

Pile: a group of winks connected directly or indirectly by squops.

Pot: (noun) the cup that is placed in the centre of the mat; (verb) to play a wink into the pot.

Scrunge: to bounce out of the pot.

Squidger: the circular disk used to propel winks.

Squop: to play a wink so that it comes to rest above another wink.

Squop-up: the situation that occurs when all winks of a partnership have been squopped. Free turns result.

Sub: to play a wink so that it ends up under another wink.

Winks: the circular counters used in the game.

Winking World: the official journal of ETwA. Published twice a year.

— CITY COLOURS —

Pittsburgh is the only US city to have professional sports teams that play in the same colours. The Pirates (baseball), Steelers (football) and Penguins (ice hockey) all wear gold, black and white.

— DEION SANDERS: A TRUE ALL-ROUNDER—

Deion Sanders is the only athlete to have played in both the World Series and the Super Bowl. In the 1992 World Series, he batted an impressive .533, a highlight of the Atlanta Braves' 4–2 defeat by the Toronto Blue Jays. He fared better in the Bowl, playing for two winning teams: the San Francisco 49ers in 1995 and Dallas Cowboys in 1996. Another Deion first: in 1989, he hit a home run for the New York Yankees and scored a touchdown for the Atlanta Falcons in the same week, the only professional player so far to have accomplished such a feat.

— WRESTLING WORLDWIDE —

Cumberland and Westmorland wrestlers stand chest to chest with their chins on their opponent's right shoulder, 'holding' each other around the body. All means bar kicking can be used for a throw. If one wrestler breaks the hold, with the other keeping it, he is declared the loser. If either man touches the ground with any part of the body other than the feet, he is the loser. If both fall together, the one who hits the ground first is the loser.

Devon and Cornwall wrestlers wear jackets, hold collar and one sleeve and must throw their opponent from a stand. A winning throw is when an opponent's hips and shoulders touch the ground. Touching the ground with parts of the body other than the feet is forbidden; two touches means disqualification.

In Glima Icelandic wrestling, competitors wear straps around their thighs, with vertical straps down each thigh. Fighters must keep hold of the opponent's harness; a winning fall is scored if an opponent is thrown to the ground. Rounds are two minutes long, with one weight category.

Kushti wrestling is practised in Iran on grass; wrestlers wear tight-fitting leather trousers. To win, a wrestler has to throw his opponent onto his back.

Pankration Ancient Greek wrestling was introduced in 648 BC. Throwing, strangling, arm-locks, biting, kicking, gouging and punching were allowed, and one of the fighters might well end up dead.

Sambo is a blend of three types of Russian folk wrestling. It takes its name from the words *samozashchita* (self-defence) and *bez oryzhya* (without weapons). Tight-fitting jackets and boots are worn; opponent must be thrown cleanly onto his back. If both fall together, contest continues on the ground with 'torture grips' – elbow and knee locks.

Schwingen is a Swiss variant in which wrestlers wear vest and leather trousers. At the start of a bout, the back of the trousers and one leg are held. For a winning throw, opponent must land on his back, with the thrower holding his trousers.

Yagli is a style of Turkish wrestling in which combatants wear long leather trousers and smear their bodies in grease. Opponents must be thrown with a shoulder and a thigh touching the ground.

— MAJOR LEAGUE BOW FOR ONE-ARMED FIELDER —

In 1945, St Louis Browns outfielder Pete Gray made his major league baseball debut. What set Gray apart was that he had only one arm, having lost his right arm when he fell off a truck as a child.

— FOOTBALLING FAKES —

Imitation is the sincerest form of flattery – at least when it comes to football club names. Barcelona were league champions in Ecuador 13 times between 1960 and 1995, while Everton have won the Chilean league three times – in 1950, 1952 and 1976. Arsenal took the title in Lesotho in 1989 and 1993, and Benfica have done the double, winning the Guinea-Bissau league four times (1977, 1982, 1988 and 1989) and the Namibian league in 1987. Not to be outdone, Liverpool won the Kenyan league in 1965 and were Namibian cup winners in 1992.

— WHEATIES…BREAKFAST OF CHAMPIONS —

Wheaties, the US cereal that markets itself as the breakfast of champions, has been putting sports stars on its boxes since 1934.

- Babe Ruth appeared in print advertisements for the cereal in the 1930s but only made his box debut in 1992.

- The first team to be honoured on the front of the package was the Minnesota Twins following their victory in the 1987 World Series.

- Michael Jordan has been on the box more than any other athlete, appearing 18 times either individually or with the Chicago Bulls.

- After the 1999 death from liver cancer of Chicago Bears running back Walter Payton, Wheaties issued a package commemorating the NFL's all-time rusher.

- In Minneapolis in 1995, Wheaties distributed package flats featuring Eiji Oue, the new director of the Minnesota Orchestra, following his debut performance.

— DRAKE WARMS UP WITH A GAME OF BOWLS —

'We still have time to finish the game and thrash the Spaniards too.' This, the most famous of bowls quotes, was said to have been uttered by Sir Francis Drake, who was playing the game on Plymouth Hoe on 18 July 1588 when the Spanish Armada was spotted. He lost the game, but the Armada was decisively beaten.

— ZAMBONI…KING OF THE RINK —

As co-owner of the Iceland rink in Paramount, California, Frank Zamboni was unimpressed by the hour or so of wasted skating time it took to clean the rink's ice by hand. He began to experiment with mechanising the process, and in 1949 produced the first Zamboni ice resurfacing machine, which shaves, cleans and resurfaces the ice as it travels. Since then, more than 7,000 have been sold and they are a familiar sight at every hockey game.

- At four resurfacings per game, a Zamboni travels an average of 3 miles (4.8km) per hockey game.

- The second Zamboni was bought by Norwegian film star and skater Sonja Henie in 1950 for her *Hollywood On Ice* revue.

- In 2001, a Zamboni was driven across Canada from St John's, Newfoundland, to Victoria, British Columbia. At 9mph (14.5kph), the journey took four months.

- The machine made its Olympic debut in the 1960 Winter Games at Squaw Valley, California. At the 2002 Winter Games in Salt Lake, Utah, 20 Zambonis were deployed.

- When a Zamboni cleans a rink, it picks up around 1,500lb (680kg) of snow and deposits about 1,200lb (544kg) of water.

— PING PONG...BUT NOT FOR TOO LONG —

The current time limit in table tennis, under which a game is 'expedited' if it lasts longer than 15 minutes, was introduced because in theory a rally between two evenly matched singles players can continue indefinitely. The 'expedite' rule avoids situations such as in the 1932 world championships, when the men's team final between Austria and Romania lasted three days.

— THE MYSTERY OF THE 10-YEAR-OLD COXSWAIN—

Before the coxed pairs rowing race at the 1900 Olympic Games in Paris, France, the Dutch team Francois Brandt and Roelof Klein decided to replace their coxswain, Hermanus Brockmann, with someone lighter. So they recruited a 10-year-old French boy to do the job – and won the race. Afterwards, though, the lad quietly slipped away and his identity remains a mystery.

— MISCELLANEOUS FOOTBALL QUOTES —

'Lalas resembles the lovechild of Rasputin and Phyllis Diller.' – *Sports Illustrated* on Alexei Lalas, US defender in the 1994 World Cup.

'I don't know if I was all that good. I never saw myself play, so how do I know?' – Sir Stanley Matthews looking back on his playing career.

'God created me to delight people with my goals.' – The ever-modest Brazilian striker Romario on his mission in life.

— MISCELLANEOUS FOOTBALL QUOTES (CONT'D) —

'There's nobody fitter at his age – except maybe Raquel Welch.' – Then Coventry manager Ron Atkinson on 39-year-old Gordon Strachan.

'One thing I've learned since becoming a manager is that in the public's mind, players win games and managers lose them.' – Then Middlesbrough player-manager Bryan Robson.

'A coach is like a winemaker. He must produce the best wine from the grapes he has available.' – Milan coach Fabio Capello after the departure of Ruud Gullit, Marco van Basten and Franck Rijkaard.

'You go in a pub and they used to have pictures of JFK and the Pope on the walls. Now it's Jack everywhere.' – Ireland striker Niall Quinn on the popularity of manager Jack Charlton in the mid-1990s.

'The World Cup wasn't won on the playing fields of England, it was won on the streets.' – Sir Bobby Charlton reflects on England's 1966 World Cup success.

'My conscience is clear. I always put my hand on my groin when I'm warming up.' – Flamengo's controversial forward Edmundo denies making an obscene gesture to rival Vasco de Gama fans.

'Soccer will never take over from baseball. Baseball's the only chance we blacks get to wave a bat at a white man without starting a riot.' – Eddie Murphy at the 1994 World Cup.

'If somebody in the crowd spits at you, you've just got to swallow it.' – Gary Lineker passes on advice given by Leicester City manager Gordon Milne.

'I loved football. I played in the morning and in the afternoon. Even when I went to bed with my wife I was training.' – Diego Maradona of Argentina.

'If people saw me walking on water you can be sure someone would say, "Look at that Berti Vogts: he can't even swim!"' – The then Germany coach Berti Vogts explains the difficulties of satisfying an expectant nation.

'He can't run, can't tackle, can't head the ball and always plays the ball sideways. The only time he goes forwards is to toss the coin. He is the crab of football.' – Ron Atkinson on his star midfielder Ray Wilkins.

'Lord Nelson, Lord Beaverbrook, Sir Winston Churchill, Sir Anthony Eden, Clement Attlee, Henry Cooper, Lady Diana. We have beaten them all. Maggie Thatcher, your boys took a hell of a beating.' – Norwegian TV commentator Borge Lillelien on his country's 2–1 win over England on 9 September 1981.

— TIC-TAC GESTURES —

Tic-tac is the secret sign language used by bookmakers at racecourses to indicate movements in the price of a horse.

— DERIVATION OF SPORTING TERMS —

Catamaran

Comes from the Tamil word *kattumaram*, which means a raft made of logs tied together with ropes. In modern sailing, it refers to a yacht with two parallel hulls. A trimaran is a yacht with two lesser hulls on either side of the main hull.

Chinaman

The cricketing word for an off-break delivered to a right-handed batsman by a left-handed bowler. Said to derive from a bowler called Ellis Achong, who was Chinese, but played for West Indies and used this type of delivery.

Scratch

This sporting term, which means to make the grade, or to meet a particular standard, originated in the *London Prize Ring Rules* of 1839, under which a round of a prize fight ended when a fighter was knocked down. After a 30-second interval, he would be given eight seconds to get to a mark scratched in the middle of the ring. If he failed, he had not 'come up to scratch' and was beaten.

— DERIVATION OF SPORTING TERMS (CONT'D) —

Cox
This rowing term is short for the word cockswain (or coxswain), the helmsman of a small light boat, which would have been referred to as a cockboat.

Cricket
Comes from the French term *criquet*, meaning goalpost.

Jodhpurs
Comes from the Indian state of Jodhpur, and the breeches worn by the maharajah when playing polo in the 1860s. His trouser style, tight at the ankle and loose up above, was brought to England with the game by British army officers.

Regatta
Originated in Venice, referring to races between gondoliers, from the Venetian dialect word *rigatta*, meaning 'confrontation'.

Source: Brewer's Dictionary Of Phrase And Fable

— POSTS UPON HIGH —

The rugby goalposts at Wednesbury, England, are the tallest in the world. Fourteen inches (35.6cm) wide at the base and set in $5\frac{1}{4}$yds^3 (4.4m^3) of concrete, the tubular steel posts stand 125ft (38.1m) high. By comparison, the posts at Twickenham are 42ft (12.8m) and the ones at Cardiff's Millennium Stadium are 55ft (16.8m) high.

— 62 GAMES ON THE BOUNCE FOR US —

Before the USA's last-second defeat by the USSR in the basketball final at the 1972 Olympic Games in Munich, the USA had gone 62 games without defeat in Olympic competition and, in fact, had never lost since the sport's introduction at the 1936 Games in Berlin.

EIGHT HOLLYWOOD STARS
— OF THE 1930s WHO PLAYED BADMINTON —

James Cagney	Claudette Colbert
Joan Crawford	Bette Davis
Douglas Fairbanks	Boris Karloff
Dick Powell	Ginger Rogers

— FASTEST GOAL IN ENGLISH SOCCER —

Claimed by Kevin Curry of D&R Motors (Midlands Regional Alliance), scored from the kick-off against Melbourne Dynamo in February 1999 with a wind-assisted ball that went into the net in 1.5 seconds.

— JUDO BELTS —

6th kyu (novice)	white	rokyu
5th kyu	yellow	gokyu
4th kyu	orange	yonkyu
3rd kyu	green	sankyu
2nd kyu	blue	nikyu
1st kyu	brown	ikkyu
1st dan (degree)	black	shodan
2nd dan	black	nidan
3rd dan	black	sandan
4th dan	black	yodan
5th dan	black	godan
6th dan	white and red	rokudan
7th dan	white and red	shichidan
8th dan	white and red	hachidan
9th dan	red	kudan
10th dan	red	judan

Notes: in Japan, there are no ranks in between white and black belt; the coloured belts were introduced in the 1930s when judo moved outside Japan. Moving up a ranking depends on the requirements of an individual school, but the principle is that the judoka must master a new set of techniques. The custom of qualified judoka wearing black belts began in 1886.

— ESCAPE TO VICTORY —

A mix of professional soccer players, footballing legends of the past and actors was assembled for the 1981 film *Escape To Victory*. The movie, which was set in a German prisoner of war camp, climaxed with a team of Allied prisoners escaping during a match against the Germans.

THE CAST LIST

Osvaldo Ardiles – won the World Cup with Argentina in 1978

Michael Caine – better known for *The Italian Job*, won an Oscar in 1999

Kazimierz Deyna – 102 caps for Poland including Olympic gold in 1972

Soren Lindsted – Dane who played for Genk and Liege in Belgium

Bobby Moore – England's World Cup-winning captain of 1966

Russell Osman – Ipswich Town and England defender

Pele – needs no introduction

Co Prins – Dutchman whose career included spells with Pittsburgh Phantoms and New York Rangers

Sylvester Stallone – plays the goalkeeper who saves a vital penalty

Mike Summerbee – championship-winning winger with Manchester City in 1968

Hallvar Thoresen – Norwegian winner of European Cup with PSV Eindhoven in 1988

Paul Van Himst – Belgium's greatest player, coached Anderlecht to UEFA Cup in 1983

John Wark – Scotland midfielder or defender, PFA Player of the Year in 1981

— RUSSIA AND THE NHL —

• USSR emerges as a force in international ice hockey when it wins gold at the 1956 Winter Olympics in Cortina, Italy. At Squaw Valley, USA, in 1960 it takes bronze and then in 1964 at Innsbruck, Austria, takes the first of what will be three consecutive golds at the Games.

- In 1972, the nominally amateur USSR team (many of the team are serving members of the Red Army) play the Summit Series against Canada, a team composed of NHL professionals. In the first game, held in Montreal, of this 'September to Remember', the Soviets send shockwaves through the sport by beating Canada 7–3. The Canadians take the eight-game series, though, by winning the final game in Moscow thanks to a Paul Henderson goal.

- In 1975, the Philadelphia Flyers become the first NHL franchise to pick a Soviet player as a draft choice when it adds Viktor Khatulov to its roster. Not surprisingly, the USSR hockey federation do not sanction him to play for the team.

- Starting in 1975 and continuing to 1991, both the Soviet national side and teams such as Red Army and Moscow Dynamo embark on annual tours of North America playing against NHL sides.

- The USSR competes in the Canada Cup, forerunner of the World Cup of Hockey, in 1976, but do not make the final. They win the Cup in 1981, beating Canada 8–1, then fail to make the 1984 final. In 1987, they are beaten by two games to one in a best-of-three final against Canada. The scoreline in each game is 6–5, and the quality of hockey in the tournament is widely reckoned to be the best ever seen.

- In 1989, the first Russian is signed to an NHL team when Sergei Priakin joins the Calgary Flames. Over the next two years, the cash-strapped Soviets allow a number of older players to join the NHL.

- The collapse of communism in 1991 opens the floodgates for NHL teams to sign players from the former USSR.

- When the New York Rangers win the 1994 Stanley Cup, Alexei Kovalev, Sergei Nemchinov, Sergei Zubov and Alexander Karpovtsev become the first Russians to have their names inscribed on the trophy.

- The Detroit Red Wings win the Stanley Cup for two years running in 1997 and 1998, with a team packed with talented Russians, most notably Igor Larionov and Sergei Fedorov. The Stanley Cup is taken to Moscow for the first time.

- There are currently more than 70 Russians playing in the NHL, as well as many other players imported from elsewhere in Europe.

— CRICKET ON HIGH —

At 7,035ft (2,144m) above sea level, the cricket pitch at Chail, northern India, is the highest in the world. It was constructed in 1893 by the Maharaja of Patiala, who ordered that a hilltop be levelled to provide the site.

— WORLD COAL-CARRYING CHAMPIONSHIPS —

What began as a £10 ($16) bet between Lewis Hartley and his drinking buddy Reggie Sedgewick in the Beehive Inn at Gawthorpe, West Yorkshire, in 1963, has now become the annual World Coal-Carrying Championships. In the competition, men carry a 50kg (110lb) sack of coal over a distance of 1km (⅔ mile). The current men's record is four minutes and six seconds. Women carry 20kg (44lb) over the same distance (current record: five minutes and five seconds).

BIZARRE EXPLANATIONS
— FOR POSITIVE DRUG TESTS —

Name	Sport	Drug	Excuse
Shane Warne	Cricket	Diuretic	Pill given to him by his mother
Dieter Baumann	Athletics	Nandrolone	Injected into his toothpaste by a third party
Gilberto Simoni	Cycling	Cocaine	In a dentist's painkiller, or perhaps in sweets his aunt brought from Colombia
No bombs	Racehorse	Caffeine and theobromine	The stableboy gave me a Mars Bar
Ben Johnson	Athletics	Testosterone	His stammer
Denis Mitchell	Athletics	Testosterone	Drinking beer and having sex
Borja Aguirrechu	Soccer	Nandrolone	Hair replacement pills

— BUDDY'S BULLFIGHTS HIT NEW JERSEY —

In 1928, amusement-park owner Buddy Brown hired 40 Mexican matadors and began staging bullfights at his park in Newark, New Jersey. More than 30,000 spectators watched the first fight and the experiment was a financial success, but it took its toll – after three weeks, Brown reported, 'One matador was dead and the other 39 were in hospital.' Bullfighting in New Jersey ceased when city officials passed a law prohibiting it in 1930.

— WAYNE GRETZKY —

Born 26 January 1961 in Brantford, Ontario, Canada, Wayne Gretzky was a phenomenon from the moment he first took to the ice. As a 10-year-old, he scored 378 goals in Brantford's atom league. When the young centre made his debut in Canada's premier junior league, the Ontario Hockey Association, he scored 70 goals for Sault Ste Marie Greyhounds to become the OHA's leading scorer for the 1977–78 season. At 17, he turned pro for the WHA's Indianapolis Racers in June 1978 and was traded to the Edmonton Oilers in November, becoming the WHA's rookie of the year in 1978–79.

The Oilers joined the NHL in the 1979–80 season and Gretzky scored his first NHL goal on 14 October 1979 (against Vancouver Canucks). Over the next 20 seasons, he broke more than 60 NHL records and led Team Canada to three Canada Cup victories. Upon his retirement on 16 April 1999, the NHL took the unprecedented step of retiring Gretzky's number 99 shirt across the league, and the Hockey Hall of Fame waived its three-year waiting period and inducted him immediately. In June 2000, Gretzky became managing partner of the Phoenix Coyotes.

NHL TEAMS
1979–80 to 1987–88	Edmonton Oilers
1988–89 to 1995–96	Los Angeles Kings
1995–96	St Louis Blues
1997–97 to 1999	New York Rangers

— WAYNE GRETZKY (CONT'D) —

SELECTED TROPHIES

Stanley Cup: 1984, 1985, 1987, 1988

Canada Cup: 1984, 1987, 1991

Art Rose Trophy (season leading scorer): 1981–87, 1990–91, 1994

Hart Memorial Trophy; (NHL Most Valuable Player): 1980–88

Conn Smythe Trophy (Stanley Cup play-offs Most Valuable Player): 1986, 1988

Lester B Pearson Award (Outstanding Player as voted by his peers): 1982–85, 1987

Lady Byng Memorial Trophy (Most Gentlemanly Player): 1980, 1991, 1992, 1994, 1999

SELECTED NATIONAL HOCKEY LEAGUE RECORDS

Gretzky played in a total of 1,487 games between 1977 and 1999

Goals:

1. Most goals: 894
2. Most goals, including play-offs: 1,016 (894 regular season, 122 play-offs)
3. Most goals, one season: 92 in 1981–82
4. Most goals, one season, including play-offs: 100 in 1983–84 (87 regular season, 13 play-offs)
5. Most goals, 50 games from start of season: 61 in 1981–82 and 1983–84
6. Most goals, one period: 4 v St Louis, 18 February 1981, 3rd period (record tied)

Assists:

7. Most assists: 1,963
8. Most assists, including play-offs: 2,223 (1,963 regular season, 260 play-offs)
9. Most assists, one season: 163 in 1985–86
10. Most assists, one season, including play-offs: 174 in 1985–86 (163 regular season, 11 play-offs)
11. Most assists, one game: 73 times: v Washington, 15 February 1980; v Chicago, 11 December 1985; v Quebec, 14 February 1986 (record tied)

Points:
12. Most points: 2,857
13. Most points, including play-offs: 3,239 (2,857 regular season, 382 play-offs)
14. Most points, one season: 215 in 1985–86
15. Most points, one season, including play-offs: 255 in 1984–85 (208 regular season, 47 play-offs)

Scoring plateaus:
16. Most 40-or-more goal seasons: 12
17. Most consecutive 40-or-more goal seasons: 12 (1979–80 to 1990–91)
18. Most 50-or-more goal seasons: 9 (record tied)
19. Most 60-or-more goal seasons: 5 (record tied)
20. Most consecutive 60-or-more goal seasons: 4 (1981–82 to 1984–85)
21. Most 100-or-more points seasons: 15
22. Most consecutive 100-or-more points seasons: 13 (1979–80 to 1991–92)
23. Most three-or-more goal games: 50
24. Most three-or-more goal games, one season: 10 in 1981–82 and 1983–84
25. Longest consecutive assist-scoring: 23 games (8 February to 24 March 1991)
26. Longest consecutive point-scoring: 51 games (5 October 1983 to 28 January 1984)

Play-off goals and assists:
27. Most play-off goals: 122
28. Most play-off assists: 260
29. Most assists, one play-off year: 31 in 1988
30. Most assists, one play-off game: 6 v LA, 9 April 1987
31. Most assists, one play-off period: 3 five times (record tied)

Play-off points:
32. Most play-off points: 382
33. Most points, one play-off year: 47 in 1985
34. Most points in final series: 13 in 1988 v Boston
35. Most points, one play-off period: 4 at LA, 12 April 1987, 3rd period (record tied)

Play-off three-or-more goal games:
36. Most three-or-more goal games: 10

— ORIGINS OF LOVE —

The tennis term for 'no score' is thought by some to have come either from the French word 'l'oeuf' meaning 'egg', which is the same shape as the oval zero. But 'love' is also used in old English as the equivalent of 'nothing', as in 'doing something for love'.

— JOHN SURTEES —

'Big John' made motorsport history in 1964 at the Mexican Grand Prix when, driving for Ferrari, he snatched victory in the Formula One World Championship from Graham Hill, becoming the first man to win world titles on two and four wheels. Surtees had won seven motorbike titles for MV Agusta (the 1956 500cc title, and the 350 and 500cc titles in 1958, 1959 and 1960) before switching to Formula One in 1960.

— THE CALCUTTA CUP —

The England and Scotland rugby union teams first competed for this trophy in 1878. The cup takes its name from the Calcutta Football Club, which was disbanded in 1877. The club's remaining funds, in Indian rupees, were melted down to produce the trophy, which is 18in (45.7cm) tall.

— SCRABBLE SCORING —

0 point	– blanks
1 point	– A, E, I, L, N, O, R, S, T, U
2 points	– D, G
3 points	– B, C, M, P
4 points	– F, H, V, W, Y
5 points	– K
8 points	– J, X
10 points	– Q, Z

— SOFTBALL... —

...was first known as indoor baseball, subsequently as 'kitten ball', then 'mush ball' before gaining its present name in 1926.

— THE DODGERS —

The Brooklyn Dodgers were originally named after their fans who had to 'dodge' trams on their way to watch the ball game. The Dodgers made history in 1947 by signing the first black player in modern baseball, Jackie Robinson, Most Valuable Player of 1949. The team moved to Los Angeles in 1958 when the New York City government refused to provide them with new facilities.

— JOCHEN RINDT —

Tragically famous as Formula One's only posthumous world champion. Born in Germany, brought up in Austria, Rindt made his F1 debut in 1965 for Cooper and was leading the championship for Lotus in 1971 when he went to Monza for the Italian Grand Prix. He died in practice on 5 September after braking too heavily into the Parabolica curve, his car dived under the crash barriers and bounced back onto the track with its front end torn away. Rindt was pronounced dead in the ambulance en route to hospital. His first place in the championship was under threat from Jacky Ickx of Ferrari, but Ickx was unable to take the series lead in the final event of the season, the US Grand Prix.

— DUKES UP —

'Dukes' as a term for fists has its origins in Cockney rhyming slang. It derives from 'Duke of Yorks', rhyming slang for 'forks', which came to mean first 'fingers', then 'hands' and then 'fists'.

— FANCY THAT —

'Fan' (as in supporter or watcher) probably derives not from fanatic but from the word fancy. In the early 19th century, bareknuckle fighting was a popular spectator sport among the gentry, who were nicknamed 'the fancy', which was often shortened to 'the fance' and hence 'fan'.

— GEORGE BEST'S GIRLFRIENDS AND WIVES —

In Britain, the Manchester United and Northern Ireland striker was as much an icon of the Swinging Sixties as The Beatles. The impression he gave was of a man who spent the week drinking champagne at the discothèque with a bevy of models on his arm but still scored brilliant goals when Saturday came. Sadly, although his eye for beautiful women never deserted him, his ability to control his drinking did. Numerous attempts at curing his alcoholism failed, culminating in a liver transplant in July 2002.

Carolyn Moore (Miss GB)	1965
Eva Haraldstad	1969
Siv Hederby	1970
Sinead Cusack	1970–71
Liz Steveley (Miss Motorway Scotland and Northern Ireland)	1971
Elisabeth Bengson	1972
Marji Wallace (Miss World)	1973
Toni Ceo	1974
Angie Best (née Janes)	1976–82 – married 1978, divorced 1988
Mary Stavin (Miss World)	1982–87
Hilary Rose	1984
Diana Janney	1984
Angela Lynn	1984–87
Kan Locke	1987
Mary Shatila	1988–94
Alex Best (née Pursey)	1994 to present – married 24 July 1995

Tanya Wild (Shopgirl who claimed to be having an affair with Best. George is reported as saying, 'The girl is a nutter and is making life hell for me. We went out about six times before my wedding and that's it.') 1995?

— BONKERS OVER CONKERS —

A university survey of 2000 found that some British schools were banning conkers because they feared that they could be used 'as offensive weapons', and the victims might sue.

— RISE AND FALL OF EDDIE THE EAGLE —

Eddie 'the Eagle' Edwards found fame as Britain's sole representative in the ski jumping competition at the Calgary Winter Olympics in 1988 because, quite frankly, he was rubbish. After finishing 56th out of 57 jumpers (the 57th was disqualified) he became a media hero in Britain and by the end of the year had earned about £385,000 ($620,000) in sponsorship. Unfortunately, the money disappeared in a string of bad investments and Edwards was declared bankrupt in 1992. He still lectures, does the occasional advert and has released records but is by no means flush with cash.

— SPORTS SUPERSTITIONS —

Lucky clothing
- Formula One driver David Coulthard's blue boxer shorts, bought for him by his Aunt Elaine, which he wore to destruction.

- England wicketkeeper Jack Russell's floppy hat. Ended up in pieces, and only his wife was allowed to do the repairs.

- Michael Jordan (a graduate of North Carolina) would always wear his blue Carolina shorts under his Chicago Bulls uniform.

Pre-match ritual
- Between Six Nations rugby games, the French lock Olivier Merle would not wear his boots. So he trained in sneakers until a team mate left a banana to get ripe in his footwear for 13 days.

— SPORTS SUPERSTITIONS (CONT'D) —

- The French defender Laurent Blanc kissed a bald man before every game of '*les bleus*' successful 1998 World Cup run: goalkeeper Fabien Barthez.

- When Goran Ivanisevic won Wimbledon in 2001, he ate in the same restaurant every evening, at the same table, eating fish soup, lamb and ice cream with chocolate sauce.

Lucky numbers
- In cricket, the number 111 is considered unlucky for batsmen. One umpire, David Shepherd, believes that the team must keep their feet off the ground until the number changes and hops on one leg as he stands watch.

Curses
- The south dressing room at Wembley stadium was held to be luckier than the north after a run of successes in the FA Cup shortly after the Second World War for teams changing in the south.

- Brazilian soccer club Vasco da Gama were cursed by a rival fan who buried a toad under the pitch, and declared that they would not win the championship for 12 years. Supporters and players spent ten years trying to dig it up.

Good luck charms
- The Dutchman Michael Boogerd won a stage of the 2002 Tour de France wearing his first tooth and that of his girlfriend on a chain round his neck, together with a four-leaf clover.

- The Rochdale Hornets rugby league prop Mickey Edwards plays with a model of Thomas the Tank Engine down his sock after he scored a hat-trick thanks to the very useful engine.

- Jack Nicklaus would always play with three pennies in his pocket.

— LEEDS LEGEND MEETS TRAGIC END —

Albert Johanneson came from South Africa to join Leeds United in 1961. The speedy winger played 197 times and scored 67 goals for the club and, in 1965, had the distinction of being the first black footballer to play in the FA Cup final, a match Leeds lost to Liverpool. Johanneson's problem was that throughout his career he had to compete against another talented winger, Eddie Gray, for a regular first-team place. In 1970, he left Leeds for a brief stint with York City, but after that he went into decline. Alcoholism and divorce took their toll and in November 1995, he was found dead at the age of 53. For two days, his body had lain undiscovered in his flat in a Leeds tower block.

— FOOTBALL WORLDWIDE —

Ball	Players	Time	Scoring
American			
Oval	11	Four quarters x 15 minutes	Touchdown: 6pts Conversion: 1pt Field goal: 3pts Safety: 2pts (to opponents)
Soccer			
Round	11	Two halves x 45 minutes	Goal: 1pt
Aussie Rules			
Oval	14–18	Four quarters x 20 minutes	Goal: 6pts Behind: 1pt
Gaelic			
Round	15	Two halves x 35 minutes	Goal: 3 pts Point: 1pt
Rugby Union			
Oval	15	Two halves x 40 minutes	Try: 5pts Conversion: 2pts Drop-goal: 3pts Penalty: 3pts
Rugby League			
Oval	13	Two halves x 40 minutes	Try: 4pts Conversion: 2pts Drop-goal: 1pt Penalty: 2pts

— NHL CONSIDER LAUNDRY ISSUES —

Teams playing at home in the NHL wear white jerseys, while visiting teams wear dark jerseys. This convention began in the 1960s when league officials decided it would be harder to keep white uniforms clean while teams were on the road.

— STELLA AUTOPSY REVEALS ALL —

Poland's Stella Walsh (Stanislawa Walasiewicz) was the first woman to break the 12-second barrier for the 100m when she recorded a time of 11.9 seconds to win gold at the 1932 Olympics in Los Angeles and, in the course of her career, set 37 athletics world records. When she was killed by robbers in 1980, an autopsy revealed that she was a hermaphrodite, with both male and female sexual organs.

— TED'S BILLION-DOLLAR TUNNEL —

In 1995, the city of Boston named a new, $2.3 billion (£1.43 billion) tunnel after one of the Boston Red Sox's most famous batters. The Ted Williams Tunnel links the city and Logan International Airport.

— JAPAN'S DAY OF SPORT —

Each year the Japanese celebrate *Taiiku no hi* (Sports Day) on the second Monday of October. The practice, which is intended to encourage ordinary people to take up healthy exercise, began during the 1964 Tokyo Olympics and became a national holiday two years later.

A SELECTION OF FORMULA
— ONE CHAMPIONS' NICKNAMES —

Name	Nickname	Explanation
James Hunt	Hunt the Shunt	Frequent crashes
Jack Brabham	Black Jack	Bad moods
Rudolph Caracciola	The Ringmeister	Expertise at the Nurburgring
Juan-Manuel Fangio	The Master	
Alain Prost	The Professor The Calculator King of Rio	Run of wins in Brazilian GPs
Ayrton Senna	The Rain Master	Expertise in the wet
Mika Hakkinen	The Flying Finn The Iceman	

— DECATHLON EVENTS —

First day: 100m • long jump • shot put • high jump • 400m
Second day: 110m hurdle • discus • pole vault • javelin • 1,500m

— HEPTATHLON EVENTS —

First day: 100m • high jump • shot put • 200m
Second day: long jump • javelin • 800m

— GLOBETROTTERS START LIFE IN CHICAGO —

The Harlem Globetrotters began not in New York but Chicago. In 1926, Abe Saperstein recruited players from Wendell Phillips High School for a new team, the Savoy Big Five, to play in Chicago's Savoy Ballroom. The idea was to attract customers to the ailing venue who would enjoy the game then dance afterwards. When that venture failed, Saperstein persuaded several of his players to form a new touring team. It made its debut the following year in Hinckley, Illinois, and Saperstein put the name 'New York Globetrotters' on players' shirts to give the impression they weren't local. The comic routines that brought worldwide fame began with the arrival of Reece 'Goose' Tatum in 1942.

— CRICKET FIELD PLACINGS —

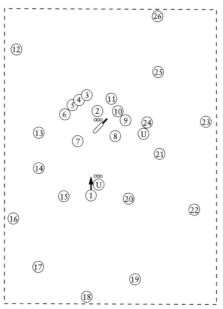

1 bowler	10 short leg	19 long-on
2 wicket-keeper	11 leg-slip	20 mid-on
3 first slip	12 third man	21 mid-wicket
4 second slip	13 cover point	22 deep mid-wicket
5 third slip	14 extra cover	23 deep square leg
6 gully	15 mid-off	24 square leg
7 silly mid-off	16 deep extra cover	25 fine leg
8 silly mid-on	17 long-off	26 long leg
9 short square leg	18 straight hit	U umpire

— DESPERDICIOS —

Perhaps the most gruesome nickname in sport is 'offal', the monicker of one Manuel Dominguez, a matador of the 19th century, who was gored in the eye during a corrida in Puerto de Santa Maria in 1857. He tore out the eye, threw it to the ground and continued the performance, living on to the healthy age of 70.

— MUSCLE, MUSCLE, MUSCLE AND...MUSCLE —

Muscle mass
Balanced muscular development
Muscle density
Muscle definition

The four basic qualities judged in body-building competitions.

— OBOLENSKY'S TRY —

One of the few rugby union players known for a single try, Prince Alexander was brought to England from his native Russia as a baby and was selected on the wing against the All-Blacks in 1936 while still technically a Russian citizen. Obolensky's second try of the game was a diagonal run from right to left, which outwitted the New Zealand defence, and which is remembered as 'Obolensky's try'.

— THE MILLE MIGLIA... —

...was a 621-mile (1,000km) open road race for cars, first run in 1926 over a course from Brescia, just to the east of Milan, to Rome and back. Organisers were the Auto Club di Brescia, who had run the first Italian Grand Prix in 1921. Among the legendary victories were those of Rudolf Caracciola, who drove the entire course single-handed in 1928, and Stirling Moss, who was partnered by the motoring journalist Denis Jenkinson in 1955. Moss mapped the entire route and recorded it on a 170ft (52m) roll of paper so that Jenkinson could guide him, with the corners divided into 'saucy ones', 'dodgy ones' and 'very dangerous ones'.

Major accidents were a feature of the event due to high speeds approaching 200mph (322kph) at times in later years and large crowds. In 1939, ten people including seven children were killed in Bologna when a Lancia lost control, while the event was abandoned after the 1958 race saw the deaths of 12 people.

— TEN GREAT UNBEATEN RUNS —

Heather McKay
Australia, Squash, 1960–77
all competitions including 16 British Opens

Celtic
Scotland, Soccer, 8 August 1964 to 13 December 1978
Scottish League Cup, 156 League Cup ties
without defeat

Alberto Ascari
Italy, Formula One, 1952–53
Nine Grand Prix wins in a row

Herb Elliott
Australia, Athletics, 12 January 1957 to 13 May 1961
36 times undefeated over a mile

Joe DiMaggio
US, Baseball, 15 May to 17 July 1941
56 safe-hitting matches in a row

Sir Gordon Richards
GB, Horse Racing, 3–5 October 1933
12 winners in 12 races at Nottingham and Chepstow
race courses

Ed Moses
US, 400m hurdles, August 1977 to June 1987
122 wins in a row

Martina Navratilova
US, Tennis, 16 January to 6 December 1984
74 women's singles matches

Aleksandr Karelin
USSR, Graeco-Roman wrestling, 1987–2000
unbeaten in international competition

US Ryder Cup team
Golf, 1959–85
unbeaten including tie in 1969

— SMOKING SOCCER SPONSORS —

The Cigarette Company of Jamaica, makers of Craven A, has been the major sponsor of soccer on the island for the past 30 years.

— PROS AND CONS —

In their book *Pros And Cons: The Criminals Who Play In The NFL*, authors Jeff Benedict and Don Yaeger claim that 21 per cent of the pro football players who took to the field in the 1996–97 season had been arrested or convicted of serious crimes. The NFL disputes their figures.

— ARGENTINA COACH BANS CHICKEN —

Carlos Bilardo, Argentina's soccer coach at the 1986 and 1990 World Cups, refused to allow his players to eat chicken because he considered it to be unlucky.

— THREE VIOLENT BASEBALL DEATHS —

• **Bugs Raymond**: a hard-drinking eccentric who once walked to the pitcher's mounds on his hands, Raymond joined the St Louis Cardinals in 1907 but his wayward habits and erratic form led to a trade the following year to the NY Giants. Flashes of brilliance weren't enough and the pitcher was released by the Giants after disappearing to a bar mid-game. In late August 1912, after an all-day binge in his native Chicago, he got into an argument and was savagely beaten, possibly with a baseball bat. He was helped back to his hotel room, where his body was discovered several days later. A post-mortem revealed he had a fractured skull.

• On 19 August 1951, **Eddie Gaedel** went into bat for the St Louis Browns for the first and only time. Browns manager Bill Veek had hired Gaedel as a publicity stunt, sending in the 3ft 7in (1.09m) midget as opening bat in the second game of a double header against the Detroit Tigers. Pitcher Bob Cain walked the diminutive batter to first base, but the next day the sport's authorities ruled

THREE VIOLENT
— BASEBALL DEATHS (CONT'D) —

that Gaedel could play no further games in the majors. Gaedel turned up in several other Veek stunts, including descending from a helicopter with three other midgets dressed as aliens to 'capture' players. On 18 June 1961, Gaedel died, aged 36, of a heart attack after being mugged in Chicago.

• Outfielder **Len Koenecke** hit the bottle after being dropped by the Brooklyn Dodgers in 1935. On 17 September of that year, while on a charter flight from Detroit to Boston, he provoked a fight with pilots William Mulqueeney and Irwin Davis that turned into a brawl. With the plane in real danger of crashing, Mulqueeney hit Koenecke over the head with a fire extinguisher, killing him instantly.

— TOE WRESTLING —

The World Toe Wrestling Championships take place each year at Ye Olde Royal Oak pub in Wetton in Derbyshire, England. Begun in 1970, the competition involves contestants sitting opposite each other on a 'toedium', locking big toes and attempting to push their opponent's foot to one side.

— NOTES ON CONKERS —

The horse chestnut tree, also known as *Æsculus hippocastanum* or *Hippocastanum vulgare* was introduced to Great Britain in the 16th century.

The first recorded game of conkers was on the Isle of Wight in 1848 and was modelled on a 15th-century game played with hazelnuts.

Ashton Conker Club organises the World Conker Championships annually on the second Sunday in October in the Leicestershire village. Entrants are not allowed to use their own conkers. Nuts are supplied for each game after being gathered and strung by the organisers. Each game lasts five minutes. If neither conker has broken, a shoot-out takes place. Each player has three sets of three hits and the one who lands most clean hits is the winner.

Random rules and facts about conkers
- If the strings tangle, the first player to call 'strings' gets an extra shot.

- If a player drops his conker, or it is knocked out of his hand the other player can shout 'stamps' and jump on it; but should its owner first cry 'no stamps' then the conker, hopefully, remains intact.

- The winner can add the loser's conker value (number of conkers it has destroyed) to the value of their conker. Thus if a 'sixer' beats a 'three-er' it becomes a 'niner'.

- The French championship is held at Abjat sur Bandiat in the Perigord region on the second Saturday in October.

- Methods of strengthening the conker include soaking in vinegar, conserving for several years in a dark cupboard, baking on a low heat (gas mark 1 [120°C] for about two hours), covering in nail varnish, covering in moisturiser.

- An Australian variant called 'bullies' is played with the seed of the quandong or wild peach tree.

— HORSERACING'S HANDICAP SYSTEM —

Used in horse-racing for 'weight-for-age' races, drawn up in the 19th century by Vice-Admiral the Honourable Henry Rous, official handicapper to the Jockey Club. Weights are in pounds, and include rider plus tack.

Horizontal scale: Months   Vertical scale: Age in years

	Jan Feb	Mar Apr	May	Jun	Jul	Aug	Nov Sep	Oct	Dec
Half mile									
2	...	...	...	...	...	105	108	111	114
3	117	119	121	123	125	126	127	128	129
4	130	130	130	130	130	130	130	130	130
5 & up	130	130	130	130	130	130	130	130	130
Six furlongs									
2	...	...	...	...	...	102	105	108	111
3	114	117	119	121	123	125	126	127	128
4	129	130	130	130	130	130	130	130	130
5 & up	130	130	130	130	130	130	130	130	130

— HORSERACING'S HANDICAP SYSTEM (CONT'D) —

One mile

2	...	...	...	...	...	...	96	99	102
3	107	111	113	115	117	119	121	122	123
4	127	128	127	126	126	126	126	126	126
5 & up	128	128	127	126	126	126	126	126	126

One and a quarter miles

2	...	...	...	...	...	...	...	...	...
3	101	107	111	113	116	118	120	121	122
4	125	127	127	126	126	126	126	126	126
5 & up	127	127	127	126	126	126	126	126	126

One and a half miles

2	...	...	...	...	...	...	...	...	...
3	98	104	108	111	114	117	119	121	122
4	124	126	126	126	126	126	126	126	126
5 & up	126	126	126	126	126	126	126	126	126

Two miles

3	96	102	106	109	112	114	117	119	120
4	124	126	126	126	126	125	125	124	124
5	126	126	126	126	126	125	125	124	124

— NIKE SWOOSH —

The ubiquitous Nike swoosh was devised by University of Oregon student Carolyn Davidson in 1964. She was originally paid $35 (£22) for the logo by company founder Phil Knight.

— WORLD'S OLDEST BOAT RACE —

The Doggett's Coat and Badge Race, first run on the Thames in London in August 1715, was named after the event's organiser, Thomas Doggett who was also manager of the nearby Drury Lane Theatre. It was taken over by the Fishmonger's Company of London on his death in 1721. It is held over a distance of 4 miles and 7 furlongs (8.05km), and runs from the Old Swan Tavern at London Bridge to the Swan Inn at Chelsea. A pub at the south side of Blackfriars Bridge, midway along the course, is named after the event.

— TOP TEN BATTERS (TOTAL HOME RUNS) —

Name	Years	At bats	Home runs	AB/HR*
Hank Aaron	23	12,364	755	16.4
Babe Ruth	22	8,399	714	11.8
Willie Mays	22	10,881	660	16.6
Barry Bonds**	17	8,335	613	13.6
Frank Robinson	21	10,006	586	17.1
Mark McGwire	16	6,187	583	10.6
Harmon Killebrew	22	8,147	573	14.2
Reggie Jackson	21	9,864	563	17.5
Mike Schmidt	18	8,352	548	15.2
Mickey Mantle	18	8,102	536	15.1

*Home Runs per At Bat ratio
**Figures up to end of 2002 season: San Francisco Giants' Barry Bonds, who in 2001 broke the record for the most home runs in a season with 73, is still an active player.*

— RAGS TO RICHES TO RAGS —

Sport is filled with stories of athletes who had it all and lost it. Poor financial advice, greedy 'friends' and a belief that the good times will never end have all contributed to their downfall, so has the difficulty of adjusting to life away from the spotlight. It's a sad fact that this trend shows no sign of abating. The NFL Players Association estimates that over the past three years 78 pro footballers have been defrauded of $42 million.

Joe Louis is the epitome of an athlete who had it all and lost it. The Brown Bomber became the first African-American heavyweight world champion since Jack Johnston when he KO'd James J Braddock on 22 June 1938 and reigned supreme for the next 11 years and 8 months. After 25 successful defences of his title, in March 1949, he retired undefeated at the age of 35. Despite earning $5 million as a fighter, within two years he didn't have a cent to show for his years in the ring. Bad debts and tax demands forced him to come out of retirement, losing in September 1950 to Ezzard Charles, his successor as champion, on points and a year later by a knock-out to Rocky Marciano. Louis's burden was lightened when President John F Kennedy wrote off his tax debts. His last years were spent as a casino host in Las Vegas, where he died on 12 April 1981.

'You, sir, are the greatest athlete in the world,' King Gustav of Sweden told **Jim Thorpe** after the American had won both the pentathlon and decathlon at the 1912 Olympics. The next year, though, Thorpe was

— RAGS TO RICHES TO RAGS (CONT'D) —

unceremoniously stripped of his medals when it was discovered that he had played minor league pro baseball in North Carolina. Public sympathy was behind Thorpe, who went on to play both football and baseball professionally. But in his later years he struggled, working variously as a labourer, movie extra and bouncer. He died penniless on 28 March 1953.

Life must have looked sweet for **Joe Pace** after winning a championship ring as a member of the Washington Bullets side that beat the Seattle Sonics in the 1978 NBA final. But addictions to drink and drugs ate all of the 6ft 11in (2.11m) basketball player's earnings and in the 1990s he was frequently homeless, drifting from Atlanta to Baltimore to Washington to Seattle. In November 2002, he was hospitalised after collapsing in a Seattle street. Doctors estimated he had consumed two six-packs of beer, a bottle of gin and an unspecified amount of crack cocaine prior to his admission to hospital.

— MICHAEL JORDAN —

Born: 17 February 1963
Height: 6ft 6in (1.98m)
Position: Guard

Selected statistics

- National Basketball Association Most Valuable Player in 1987–88, 1990–91, 1991–92, 1995–96, 1997–98

- Picked for All-NBA First Team ten times: 1986–87 to 1992–93, 1995–96 to 1997–98

- Chosen as one of the '50 Greatest Players in NBA History' in 1996

- Winner of six NBA championship titles with the Chicago Bulls: 1990–91, 1991–92, 1992–93, 1995–96, 1996–97 and 1997–98

- Picked nine times for the NBA All-Defensive First Team: 1987–88 to 1992–93, 1995–96 to 1997–98

- Named NBA Defensive Player of the Year in 1988

- Named NBA Rookie of the Year in 1985

- At the end of the 2001–02 season ranked first in NBA history in scoring average (31 points per game)

- Shares the NBA record with Wilt Chamberlain for most consecutive seasons leading the league in scoring (seven, 1986–87 to 1992–93)

- Holds the NBA record for most consecutive games scoring in double-digits (842)

The phenomenon

- In 1978, Jordan was dropped for a while from the school basketball team at Laney High School in Wilmington, North Carolina. After graduation, he went to the University of North Carolina, where he scored the winning basket in the 1982 NCAA championship game.

- He was a member of the gold medal-winning US squad at the 1984 Olympics, leading the team's scoring with an average of 17.1 points per game. When professional sportsmen were allowed into the Games, he played at the Olympics again in 1992 as a member of the victorious US 'Dream Team'.

- Picked third overall in the 1984 NBA draft by the Chicago Bulls after the Portland Trailblazers decide not to select him. Oops.

- On turning pro in 1984, he signed a sponsorship deal with Nike worth $2.5 million over five years. The Air Jordan line of shoes was introduced the following year; Nike sold $110 million worth of them in the first year.

- Film director Spike Lee directed the 1987 'Hang Time' advert for Nike that helped turn Jordan into an international icon.

- In 1992, copies of three cheques signed by Jordan, totalling $108,000, were found in the possession of murder victim Eddie Dow. Jordan later admitted the cheques were written to pay off gambling debts.

- On 13 August 1993, Jordan's father, James, was found dead in his car in South Carolina. He had been murdered.

- Jordan announced his retirement from basketball on 6 October 1993. He signed to play minor league baseball for the Birmingham Barons for the 1994 season, but did not shine.

— MICHAEL JORDAN (CONT'D) —

- The Chicago Bulls retired his number 23 shirt in November 1994. When Jordan decided to make a comeback for the team in March 1995, he initially wore number 45 but soon reverted to his famous 23.

- In 1996, he made his movie debut in *Space Jam*, co-starring with Bugs Bunny, Marvin the Martian and Porky Pig.

- For the 1996–97 season, Jordan signed a one-year $30 million contract with the Chicago Bulls.

- Jordan is a keen golfer with a handicap of four.

- Besides Nike, who by the mid-1990s were paying Jordan an estimated $20 million a year, Jordan has endorsed Gatorade, Ball Park frankfurters, Hanes, McDonald's, Oakley, Wheaties, Wilson and MCS World Com. He also has his own signature line of Michael Jordan cologne and Brand Jordan clothing line. Such sponsorship deals are estimated to earn him more than $42 million per year.

- When Jordan announced his second retirement in June 1999, Nike's stock fell 5.3 per cent on the New York Stock Exchange.

- In 1996 Jordan featured in *People Magazine*'s '10 Best Dressed' list.

- *Fortune* magazine estimates that Jordan's superstar status was worth $10 billion to the NBA in extra revenue. In 1985, for example, CBS's four-year contract for the rights to televise games cost the company $188 million. In 1989, they had to pay $600 million.

- Jordan made a second comeback in 2001, playing for the Washington Wizards.

- In a mid-1990s Associated Press survey, Jordan tied with God as the person African-American schoolchildren most admired.

— THE WORDS OF THE HAKA —

Ka mate! Ka mate! Ka ora! Ka ora!
I die! I die! I live! I live!

Ka mate! Ka mate! Ka ora! Ka ora!
I die! I die! I live! I live!

Tenei te tangata puhuru huru
This is the hairy man

Nana nei i tiki mai
Who fetched the Sun

Whakawhiti te ra
And caused it to shine again

A upa...ne! ka upa...ne!
One upward step! Another upward step!

A upane kaupane whiti te ra!
One upward step, another...the Sun shines!!

Hi !!!

— ALL BLACKS ADOPT THE HAKA —

The first haka in an international rugby match was performed by the New Zealand Native Team which toured Britain in 1888. This team was also the first to wear a black outfit with the Silver Fern emblem on the left breast. The term 'All-Blacks' was coined when the first official New Zealand touring side visited Britain in 1905.

Haka is the generic term for Maori dance; the haka performed by the All-Blacks derives from a celebratory song said to have been composed by the chief Te Rauparaha in the 1820s after he was saved from warriors of a rival tribe by the wife of a neighbouring chief (the 'hairy man' of the song) who hid him under her skirt.

— GUIDELINES FOR WHIPPING —

'The whip should be used for safety, correction and encouragement only and the Stewards of the Jockey Club therefore advise all riders to consider the following good ways of using the whip, which are not exhaustive:

- Showing the horse the whip and giving it time to respond before hitting it.

- Using the whip in the backhand position for a reminder.

- Having used the whip, giving the horse a chance to respond before using it again.

- Keeping both hands on the reins when using the whip down the shoulder in the backhand position.

- Using the whip in rhythm with the horse's stride and close to its side.

- Swinging the whip to keep a horse running straight.'

From the Jockey Club guidelines on use of the whip.

— CUBS IN HIBERNATION —

The Chicago Cubs were one of the eight founder members of baseball's National League, which was formed at an 1876 meeting held in New York's Grand Central Hotel. The team, though, hasn't won a World Series since 1908 and its most recent appearance in the sport's most important contest was back in 1945 when the Cubs lost to the Detroit Tigers of the American League.

— TOUR DE FRANCE RECORDMEN —

The world's greatest cycle race has been won five times by just four cyclists:

Jacques Anquetil	France	1957, 1961, 1962, 1963, 1964
Eddy Merckx	Belgium	1969, 1970, 1971, 1972, 1974
Bernard Hinault	France	1978, 1979, 1981, 1982, 1985
Miguel Indurain	Spain	1991, 1992, 1993, 1994, 1995
Lance Armstrong	USA	1999, 2000, 2001, 2002, 2003

— DOUBLE TOUR WINNERS —

The most heroic feat of stamina on two wheels,
however, is winning the Tours of Italy and France
in the same year, as the two events, of similar
distance, take place within the space of just
three months.

Fausto Coppi	Italy	1949, 1952
Anquetil		1964
Merckx		1970, 1972, 1974
Hinault		1982
Stephen Roche	Ireland	1987
Indurain		1992, 1993
Marco Pantani	Italy	1998

— THE DAVIS CUP IS BORN —

'If team matches between players from different parts of
the same country arouse such great interest and promote
such good feeling, would not international contests have
even wider and far-reaching consequences?' Thus mused
Dwight Filley Davis, a Harvard student who had just won
the 1899 intercollegiate tennis singles title. To test his
theory, he lashed out $700 (£435) on a silver trophy in his
graduation year, 1900.

A Great Britain team was invited to Longwood Cricket
Club to take on Davis and an all-Harvard team over
three days of competition, with two singles matches on
the first day, a doubles match on the second, and two
more singles matches on the third day. Harvard won the
first three matches, and the fourth game was called off
with the second set tied, beginning the tradition that play
ends when either country wins three matches.

By 1920, there was no space on the original bowl for any
more results, so Davis spent $400 (£250) on a large silver
tray and after his death in 1945, the trophy was renamed
the Davis Cup in his memory. Davis became president of
the US Lawn Tennis Association in 1923 and served under
President Calvin Coolidge as US Secretary of War from
1925–29 and later as Governor General of the Philippines.

— RECORD MONACO GP WINNERS —

6 Ayrton Senna, Brazil

Lotus-Honda	1987
McLaren-Honda	1989, 1990, 1991, 1992
McLaren-Ford	1993

5 Graham Hill, GB

BRM	1963, 1964, 1965
Lotus-Ford	1968, 1969

5 Michael Schumacher, Germany

Benetton-Ford	1994
Benetton-Renault	1995
Ferrari	1997, 1999, 2001

4 Alain Prost, France

McLaren-TAG	1984, 1985, 1986
McLaren-Honda	1988

— ROBBIE BURNS ON CURLING —

When winter muffles up his cloak,
And binds the mire like a rock;
When to the loughs the curlers flock
    Wi gleesome speed,
Wha will they station at the cock?
    Tam Sampson's deid!

He was the king o' a' the core,
To guard, or draw, or wick a bore,
Or up the rink like Jehu roar
    In time o' need;
But now he lags on Death's 'hog-score',
    Tam Sampson's dead!

— ALL-AMERICAN SOAP BOX DERBY —

The brainchild of US journalist Myron E Scott, the first All-American Soap Box Derby was held in Dayton, Ohio in 1934. It was won by Robert Turner of Muncie, Indiana. The following year the race moved to Akron, where it is still held each year. Chevrolet, the race's first sponsor, gave a $2,000 (£1,200) college scholarship to winner Maurice Bale of Anderson, Indiana. The racers who came second and third received cars as prizes.

— 'JOLTIN' JOE DIMAGGIO' —

The song 'Joltin' Joe DiMaggio', which tells the story of the baseball legend's 56-game hitting streak, was written in 1941 by New York disc jockey Alan Courtney and recorded by band leader Les Brown.

Hello Joe, whatta you know?
We need a hit so here I go.
Ball one (Yea!)
Ball two (Yea!)
Strike one (Booo!)
Strike two (Kill that umpire!)
A case of Wheaties

He started baseball's famous streak
That's got us all aglow
He's just a man and not a freak,
Joltin' Joe DiMaggio.

Joe, Joe DiMaggio
We want you on our side

He tied the mark at forty-four
July the 1st you know
Since then he's hit a good twelve more
Joltin' Joe DiMaggio

Joe, Joe DiMaggio
We want you on our side

From coast to coast that's all you'll hear
Of Joe the one man show
He's glorified the horsehide sphere
Joltin' Joe DiMaggio

Joe, Joe DiMaggio
We want you on our side

— 'JOLTIN' JOE DIMAGGIO' (CONT'D) —

He'll live in baseball's Hall of Fame
He got there blow by blow
Our kids will tell their kids his name
Joltin' Joe DiMaggio

We dream of Joey with the light brown plaque
Joe, Joe DiMaggio
We want you on our side

And now they speak in whispers low
Of how they stopped our Joe
One night in Cleveland Oh Oh Oh
Goodbye streak DiMaggio

— RED RUM —

The greatest Grand National winner of all time, Red Rum, took his name
from the last three letters of his dam and sire Mared and Quorum.

— THE ORIGINS OF THE HAT-TRICK —

Apparently originated in cricket during the 19th
century. There are two explanations. One is that it came
from a match when a hatter offered a bowler-hat to any
bowler taking wickets with three consecutive balls. The
other is that if a bowler managed the feat he was
allowed to take a hat round the ground to collect money
from the crowd. In soccer, the original meaning was
three consecutive goals by any single player, uninterrupted
by a goal from a team-mate.

— BLUE IS THE COLOUR FOR ITALY —

Italian national sides are always known as *azzurri* – the azure blues – and
always wear kit based on sky blue, in spite of the fact that the national flag
is red, white and green. That's because the Italian flag was adopted only in
1946, after the Second World War, while the blue dates back to the 19th
century, when it was the colour of the house of Savoy, the Italian monarchs.

— THE GRAND NATIONALS THAT NEVER WERE —

Both the 1993 and 1951 Grand Nationals turned into farce by starters' errors. The 1993 race had two false starts when the starter's tape failed to rise above the horses, but in the second the official responsible for stopping the field failed to see the starter's red flag signalling the false start, and let them go. Eight jockeys had seen the signal and stopped their mounts, while a ninth, Richard Dunwoody on Won't Be Gone Long, was half-strangled by the tape. An attempt to stop the race using traffic cones failed when the jockeys assumed the officials were animal rights protesters. The race was declared void, unlike the 1951 event, where the tape was released with half the field pointing the wrong way, and in the chaos that followed only two were left standing including the winner, Royal Tan.

— MARTINA NAVRATILOVA IN FIGURES —

331 weeks at world No1, second only to Steffi Graf (373)

167 singles tournament victories as of 1 June 2003

163 doubles tournament victories as of 1 June 2003

18 Grand Slams

9 Wimbledon titles

109 unbeaten doubles matches with Pam Shriver

1,000,000: her dollar earnings in 1982, the first woman athlete to break six figures

30 years as a professional tennis player (1973–2003)

— BABE BRINGS NEW JOY TO YANKEES —

The great George Herman 'Babe' Ruth holds the record for most total bases achieved in a season with his tally of 457 in 1921. When Ruth joined the New York Yankees, the team had never won an American League pennant. During his years with the team, from 1919 to 1934, they won seven titles and four world series (1923, 1927, 1928 and 1932).

— ICE HOCKEY'S HARDEST MEN —

They call Philadelphia 'the city of brotherly love' but no one told Dave 'The Hammer' Schultz that when he joined the Philly Flyers at the start of the 1972–73 ice hockey season. The 6ft 1in (1.85m), 195lb (88.5kg) Schultz quickly established a reputation as the NHL's most fearsome enforcer, spending 259 minutes in the sinbin in his rookie year, 348 minutes in 1973–74, 472 minutes in 1974–75 (still a record for the most penalty minutes in a single season) and 405 minutes in 1977–78. He's the only player in NHL history to break the 400 penalty minutes mark twice, and between 1972 and 1975 accounted for 22 per cent of all penalty minutes awarded against the Flyers. The fans loved it, as the Flyers (nicknamed the Broad Street Bullies for their intimidating tactics) won the Stanley Cup two seasons running in 1973–74 and 1974–75.

— SCHULTZ HAMMERED AGAIN —

Schultz also holds the record for the most penalty minutes clocked up in a Stanley Cup play-off game. When the Flyers met the Toronto Maple Leafs on 22 April 1976, Schultz spent 42 minutes in the bin, the result of one minor penalty, two five-minute major penalties, a ten-minute misconduct and a double game misconduct.

In that game, Schultz went head-to-head with another fearsome enforcer, the Maple Leaf's Dave 'Tiger' Williams. In a 14-season career, spanning 1974 to 1988, Williams spent a total of 3,966 minutes in the sinbin, another NHL record.

— STEAMING TO GLORY —

Sweden hosts an annual sauna championships. Ari Petrof spent five hours and ten minutes in a 212°F (100°C) sauna to win the title in 2003.

— TRIPLE CROWNS —

Eleven horses have won the US Triple Crown of the Preakness Stakes at Pimlico, Baltimore, the Belmont Stakes, and the Kentucky Derby at Louisville:

1919 Sir Barton
1930 Gallant Fox
1935 Omaha
1937 War Admiral
1941 Whirlaway
1943 Court Fleet
1946 Assault
1948 Citation
1973 Secretariat
1977 Seattle Slew
1978 Affirmed

Fifteen horses have won the old British Triple Crown of the 2000 Guineas at Newmarket, Epsom Derby and St Leger at Doncaster:

1853 West Australian
1865 Gladiator
1866 Lord Lyon
1886 Ormonde
1891 Common
1893 Isinglass
1897 Galtee More
1899 Flying Fox
1900 Diamond Jubilee
1903 Rock Sand
1915 Pommera
1917 Gay Crusader
1918 Gainsborough
1935 Bahram
1970 Nijinsky II

— CROSSBARS INTRODUCED IN SOCCER —

The wooden crossbar on the football goal was first introduced in 1875. Before that, a belt was stretched between the two uprights to mark the top. Goals were recorded by cutting a small notch in the uprights. Hence the expression 'to score a goal'.

— THE CRESTA RUN —

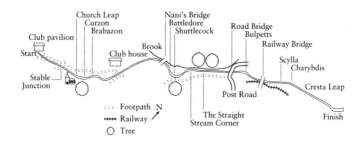

— JAMES FRANCIS THORPE —

Part Algonquin Indian, part Irish, born 1888, died 1953. Perhaps the best all-round athlete ever, excelling at five sports.

Football: All American half-back in 1911–12. Professional footballer from 1921–25, with a fine hip-twist and strong drop-kick.

Baseball: Played for New York Giants in National League from 1913–20.

Pentathlon: Won the 1912 Olympic gold at Stockholm, best in four of five disciplines.

Decathlon: Won the 1912 Olympic gold at Stockholm, 700 points clear of runner-up.

Also placed fourth equal in the high jump at Stockholm.

Thorpe was stripped of his medals by the IOC in 1913, after it was revealed that he had played professional baseball in 1909 (see also pp139–40).

— IN SPORTING MEMORIAM —

'A Gentle Man and a Gentleman'
Jack Dempsey

'May
That Divine Spirit
That Animated
BABE RUTH
to Win the Crucial
Game of Life
Inspire the Youth
of America'

'Respect this place, this hallowed ground. A legend here,
his rest has found. His feet would fly, our spirits soar.
He earned our love for evermore.'
Red Rum, buried next to the Aintree winning post

'World champion bicycle racer who came up the hard
way without hatred in his heart, an honest, courageous
and god-fearing, clean-living, gentlemanly athlete. A
credit to his race who always gave out his best. Gone
but not forgotten.'
Marshall W 'Major' Taylor, champion sprint cyclist

'Deeply regretted by numerous friends and all golfers, he
thrice in succession won the championship belt and held
it without rivalry and yet without envy, his many
amiable qualities being no less acknowledged than his
golfing achievements.'
*Young Tom Morris, golfer, triple winner of British
Open, died 25 December 1875*

'His body ached, his legs grew tired, but still he would
not give in.'
Tom Simpson, British world champion cyclist

'Ad maiora ultra vitam'
(To the better things beyond life)
On the Ferrari family tomb where Enzo Ferrari is buried

— HATS OFF FOR EARLY TRAP SHOOT —

Clay pigeon, or trap, shooting
derived from shooting contests
in which live pigeons were
covered with the shooters' hats
before being released. When
this was made illegal, glass balls
were used, sometimes filled
with feathers. In 1880 'pigeons'
were first made out of river silt
and pitch.

— IRONMAN RIPKEN —

Baseball's major league Ironman record is currently held
by Cal Ripken Jr, who played 2,632 games consecutively
between 30 May 1982 and 19 September 1998.

— SHUTTLECOCK —

Olympic regulations governing badminton state that the
shuttlecock must have 14 feathers.

— WORLD LIZARD RACING CHAMPIONSHIPS —

Eulo in Queensland, Australia, is home of
the annual world lizard racing
championships, which are held every
August. A plaque on a granite rock on the
left-hand side of the Paroo track where
the races are held is one of sport's more
unusual memorials. It reads: 'Cunnamulla
Eulo Festival of Opals. "Destructo",
champion racing cockroach, accidentally
killed at this track (24 August 1980) after
winning the challenge stakes against
"Wooden Head", champion racing lizard
1980. Unveiled 23 August 1981.'

— ICE HOCKEY PENALTIES —

Two minutes	charging, elbowing, tripping, body checking, high sticks, shooting out of the rink, falling on the puck
Five minutes	fighting
Ten minutes	abusive language
Match penalty	deliberately injuring or attempting to injure an opponent

— FATAL CONSEQUENCES OF PLAYING TENNIS —

Tennis, played widely by the medieval aristocracy, was not without its dangers. Louis X of France (1316), Henry I of Castile (1217) and Philip I of Spain (1506) all died of chills after playing the game, while Charles VIII of France suffered fatal head injuries in 1498 from hitting his head on a low doorway on the way to watch a game at the royal castle of Amboise. Most bizarrely of all, however, James I of Scotland was unable to escape assassins in 1437 because the escape route out of his castle, a drain, had been blocked to prevent losing tennis balls.

— NON-AMERICAN WINNERS OF THE INDY 500 —

1913	Jules Goux, France
1914	Rene Thomas, France
1915	Ralph DePalma, Italy
1916	Dario Resta, Italy
1920	Gaston Chevrolet, France
1946	George Robson, England
1965	Jim Clark, Scotland
1966	Graham Hill, England
1969	Mario Andretti, Italy
1989/93	Emerson Fittipaldi, Brazil
1990/97	Arie Luyendyk, Netherlands
1995	Jacques Villeneuve, Canada
1999	Kenny Brack, Sweden
2000	Juan Montoya, Colombia
2001/2	Helio Castroneves, Brazil
2003	Gil De Ferran, Brazil

— FIRST AFRICAN-AMERICAN IN PRO BASKETBALL —

Although records are sketchy, Harry H 'Bucky' Lew was probably the first African-American to play professional basketball. Born in Lowell, Massachusetts, in 1884, Lew played his first pro game for Lowell of the New England League when he came on as a substitute against Marlboro in 1902. Although subjected to a torrent of name-calling and abuse in that game and many others, Lew played professionally for more than 20 years. After the New England League disbanded in 1906, he formed his own team, Bucky Lew's Travelling Five and retired from the sport in 1926 at the age of 42.

It wasn't until 1950 that the first African-Americans played in the NBA. That year saw the arrival of Chuck Cooper (Boston Celtics), Earl Lloyd (Washington Capitols) and Nathaniel 'Sweetwater' (New York Knicks).

— GOLFING FERRETS —

Golden ferret When a golfer holes a bunker shot.
Sandy ferret When a golfer holes up and down from a bunker.

— AVIATOR HONOURED BY STADIUM —

The Stade Roland Garros in Paris, home of the French Open Tennis championship, is named after a French pioneer of air travel. Garros was the first man to fly over the Mediterranean in 1913. He was also the inventor of the system for firing machine guns through an aeroplane's propellers which made aerial warfare possible.

— WILLIAM WEBB ELLIS —

'This stone commemorates the exploit of William Webb Ellis, who, with a fine disregard for the rules of football as played at the time, first took the ball in his arms and ran with it, thus originating the distinctive feature of the Rugby game. AD 1823.'

Wording of a plaque at Rugby school in honour of the schoolboy generally, but probably erroneously, credited with founding rugby.

— BRICKYARD...HOME OF THE INDY 500 —

The Indianapolis Motor Speedway, home of the Indy 500, is known as the 'Brickyard' because shortly after its opening in 1909 its original surface of crushed rocks and tar broke up and the track was repaved with 3.2 million bricks, many of which remain under today's asphalt surface.

— THE BLIND BOMBER —

George Glamack played a major part in the University of North Carolina basketball squad winning the Southern Conference championship in 1940. As captain of the 1941 team, he led the team to the Southern Conference regular-season title and to UNC's first appearance in the NCAA tournament. In both years, the 6ft 6in (1.98m) tall player was named All-Southern Conference, All-America and National Player of the Year by the Helms Foundation. What set Glamack apart, though, was his eyesight. Nicknamed the Blind Bomber, he was so shortsighted that he could barely make out the hoop and used the court markings as guides to navigate his way around. Equipped with a deadly hook shot, he averaged 20.6 points per game in 1941, a highly impressive figure for the time.

— OFFICIALS ON THE RUN —

According to current FIFA fitness guidelines, referees can be expected to run up to 8 miles (12.9km) during a single soccer match. Linesmen must be able to run just over 4 miles (6.4km).

— THE BEER BALL LEAGUE —

Founded in 1882, during its nine-year existence the American Association was a serious challenger to the National League's role as baseball's major league. Between 1884 and 1890 the champions of the AA and the NL met in a 'world championship' series. The AA was nicknamed the Beer Ball League as brewery owners sat on the board of six of its teams and the league allowed beer to be sold at games.

— PAU HOSTS FIRST GRAND PRIX —

The first automobile race to be called a Grand Prix was held in the city of Pau in the Pyrenees of southern France in 1901. It was won by Henri Fournier, a pioneer of motor-racing who, in November of the same year, set a world automobile speed record of 1 mile (1.6km) in 52 seconds. The same street circuit around Pau was used in 1930 as the venue for the first official French Grand Prix, contested by Formula Libre cars. In 1933 the track layout was altered – and it remains more or less unchanged today – to a circuit characterised by hairpin bends and very short straights. Pau is currently used for Formula Three races but staged Formula One events between 1950 and 1957 and again from 1961 to 1963.

— ORIGINS OF LACROSSE —

'Born of the North American Indian, christened by the French and adopted and raised by the Canadians.' The Native American Indian version of the game of lacrosse was known as *baggataway*, and was played by at least 48 Indian tribes in southern Canada and the US. The French name for the game comes from the shape of the racket, which looks like a bishop's crozier ('crosse' in French). The Indians used a stick curved at one end to form a loop and used a ball made of deerskin sewn with deer sinews. The goals were marked by trees, about 500yds (457m) apart, and the game was used as a means of training young warriors. The first record of a white colonist playing the game is in 1844.

— SHAKESPEAREAN SOCCER —

Shakespeare was a football fan. In Act II, Scene I of *The Comedy of Errors*, when the slave Dromio of Ephesus is ordered by his mistress, Adriana, to fetch his master, he complains, 'Am I so round with you as you with me, that like a football you do spurn me thus? You spurn me hence and he will spurn me hither: if I last in this service, you must case me in leather.'

— THE LACE-FREE BALL TAKES SHAPE —

In the mid-19th century Charles Goodyear first put an air-filled rubber chamber in a leather covering to create a ball. The lace-free ball, though, was invented in the 1930s by three Argentinians (Tossolini, Valbonesi and Polo), who made a valve that allowed the chamber to be injection-filled.

— BRIEF GUIDE TO SUMO CEREMONY —

The *gyoji* (referee) sings the names of the *sumotori* (wrestlers), who wear the *mawashi* (a belt made of a strip of silk about 33ft [10m] long, folded in six and wound round the waist), from which dangle *sagari* (tassels). Their hair is tied into a knot known as *mageo-icho-mage* for higher ranked, *chonmage* for the lesser fighters. The sumotori go their corners of the *dohyo* (ring), which is

— BRIEF GUIDE TO SUMO CEREMONY (CONT'D) —

delineated by braids of rice straw. There, they stamp the
ground and are given water by another sumotori (the
winner of the previous match, or one who is waiting his
turn), rinse out their mouths, wipe their lips and perhaps
their armpits with white paper, sprinkle salt on the dohyo
(to ward off evil spirits) and clap their hands. They show
the palms of their hands to confirm they are not holding
weapons, and move to the middle of the ring, where they
stamp and stare at one another before combat begins.

— THE UNSER DYNASTY —

Between them the Unsers count eight victories in the Indy
500. Four of these triumphs go to joint record-holder Al
Unser Sr (1970, 1971, 1978 and 1987); two to Al Sr's
brother Bobby (1975 and 1981); and two to Al Unser Jr
(1992 and 1994), who is the first second-generation Indy
champion. Al Sr's father Jerry and uncles, Louis and Joe,
were also drivers. Joe lost his life while test-driving a
FWD Coleman Special on the Denver highway in 1929.
Jerry was the first Unser to start the Indy 500, finishing
31st in the 1958 race, but was killed in a practice run the
following year. Also on the Indy roster are Jerry's son,
Johnny, and Bobby's son, Robby.

— SHUFFLEBOARD —

According to the rules adopted by the US National Shuffleboard
Association, the maximum permitted length of a cue is 6ft 3in (1.9m).

— OLD BOWLS —

The oldest bowls club in the world is believed to be in
Southampton, England, where the green was laid in 1187, coming
into regular use for bowling in 1299. The club hosts the oldest
bowls tournament in the world, the Knighthood, held annually
since 1 August 1776. The winner receives a 'Knighthood' on the
green, and the title 'sir'.

— ONLY THE BALLS BOUNCE —

The world's most prolific streaker is Mark Roberts, 39, who claims almost 200 nude appearances at major events, including: the Commonwealth Games 100m in 2002; the Champions League Final in 2002; the FA Cup final; the Wimbledon men's final; the Rugby World Cup final; the Grand National; and the London Marathon. Roberts' trademark is writing a slogan on his back. His body famously read: 'Only the Balls Bounce' when interrupting Anna Kournikova at Wimbledon (the slogan was the same as that of her sports bra sponsor). Asked what he does in his spare time, Roberts replied: 'Shave my bum, shave my legs, buff my willy and go to the pub.'

— CLELAND ON TENNIS —

'The tennis court, whereby I would have you to recreate your mind, and exercise your body sometimes: for besides pleasure it preserveth your health, in so far as it moves every part of the body. Nevertheless I approve not those who are ever in the tennis court…and heat themselves so much that they rather breed than expel sickness: nor yet commend I those who rail at the Tennis-keeper's score, and that have banded away the greater part of their wealth in playing great and many sets.'

James Cleland, *The Institution of a Young Noble Man*, 1607

— HOW TO TEST BOWLS —

In 1928, the International Bowls Board, which has since become the World Bowls Board laid down the rules for the testing of bowls. The bowls should run for approximately 28ft (8.53m), the maximum draw being about 4ft 6in (1.37m). The most important addition to the specifications is that the running time of a bowl should be 12–15 seconds.

— GREY DAY FOR STAMPEDERS —

In 1995 the Baltimore Stallions became the first US-based team to win Canadian football's Grey Cup when they beat the Calgary Stampeders 37–20 in Regina, Saskatechewan. The game also saw the longest field goal in Grey Cup history – a 53yds (48.5m) kick by Baltimore's Carlos Huerta.

— PLATE MEASUREMENTS —

The home plate in baseball is 17in (43.2cm) wide.

— ALI MAKES SILENT DEBUT —

Then known as Cassius Clay, Muhammad Ali made his movie debut in the 1962 film *Requiem For A Heavyweight*, starring Anthony Quinn – himself a former professional fighter. Ali appears early on in a non-speaking role as 'ring opponent'. Two years later, at the age of 22, he was crowned heavyweight champion of the world after defeating Sonny Liston in Miami.

— RACERS BARE ALL —

Each year the Lake Como Family Nudist Resort in Lutz, Florida, holds a Dare to Go Bare 3-mile (5km) running race that attracts 250–400 nude participants.

— A TRIO OF GOLFING MASTERS —

Tiger Woods, Jack Nicklaus and Arnold Palmer all won three Masters titles in their eighth start at the Augusta, Georgia, tournament.

— SONJA SKATES HER WAY TO HOLLYWOOD —

Norwegian figure skater Sonja Henie won the women's world championship title for ten consecutive years starting in 1927. Her success on ice led to international fame and a career in Hollywood, where she appeared in movies such as the 1952 version of *The Count Of Monte Cristo* as well as many films, including *Thin Ice* and *Snow Fun*, which were tailored to show off her skating skills.

— GURNEY WINS DAYTONA IN BROKEN-DOWN CAR —

Motor racing's Dan Gurney won the 1962 Daytona three-hour race even though his Arciero Lotus 19's engine died a few minutes before the end of the timed race. Gurney's lead was large enough for him to stop the car on the banking just before the finish and allow it to coast across the line to take the chequered flag. The American went on to race successfully in Formula One, winning four Grand Prix before his retirement in 1970.

— OLYMPIC RECORDMEN —

Three athletes in Olympic history have won the same event four times:

Carl Lewis (USA),
long jump: 1984, 1988, 1992, 1996

Al Oerter (USA)
discus: 1956, 1960, 1964, 1968

Paul Elvstrom (Denmark)
single-handed Olympic yachting: 1948, 1952, 1956, 1960*

Lewis is also one of just four athletes who have taken nine gold medals. Their respective hauls are:

Lewis – *1984*: 100m, 200m, 4 x 100m relay, long jump. *1988*: 100m (after disqualification of Ben Johnson), long jump. *1992*: long jump, 4 x 100m relay. *1996*: long jump.

Paavo Nurmi (Finland) – *1920*: 10,000m, cross-country, team cross-country. *1924*: 1,500m, 5,000m, cross-country, team cross-country, 3000m. *1928*: 10,000m. His victories in the 1,500m and 5,000m in Paris came less than an hour apart on the same day (10 July 1924).

Mark Spitz (USA) – *1968*: 4 x 100m relay; 4 x 200m relay. *1972*: 200m butterfly, 4 x 100m freestyle relay, 200m freestyle, 100m butterfly, 4 x 200m freestyle relay, 100m freestyle, medley relay. (See 'The Spitz Blitz' p95.)

— OLYMPIC RECORDMEN (CONT'D) —

Larisa Latynina (Russia) – *1956*: gymnastics all-around, floor, horse vault, team. *1960*: all-around, floor, team. *1964*: floor, team. Latynina also won a total of nine silver and bronze medals, giving her the distinction of having won the most medals of any athlete in Olympic history.

Ray Ewry of the US won eight Olympic gold medals in 1900, 1904 and 1908. However, he competed in events that are no longer held; that is, the standing high jump, the standing long jump and the standing triple jump. The former polio sufferer also landed golds in the high and triple jumps at the Intercalated Games of 1906.

*Elvstrom also competed in the 1984 Games in the Tornado catamaran with his daughter Trine, narrowly finishing fourth.

— HORSERACING ON ICE —

Every year, usually in February, horseraces are held on the surface of a frozen lake at St Moritz, Switzerland. The 'White Turf' races were originally staged by local people to mark the end of the skiing season but now form part of a range of winter equestrian events, including show-jumping and polo, at the resort.

— GOLF'S OLDEST MAJOR —

The British Open is the oldest of golf's Major tournaments. It was first played at the Prestwick Club in 1860, with the stated intention of deciding the 'champion golfer of the world'.

— AUSTINS POWER TO WIMBLEDON TITLE —

In 1980 John and Tracey Austin became the first brother and sister pairing to win the mixed doubles competition at Wimbledon.

— WREN REMEMBERED —

'Garrincha
Joy of Pau Grande
Joy of Mage*
Joy of Brazil
Joy of the World

He was a sweet child
He spoke with the birds'

Inscription on memorial in Pau Grande, Brazil, to Garrincha, legendary footballer of the 1950s and early 1960s. The mesmerising winger was a member of the Brazil teams that won the World Cup in 1958 and 1962. Christened Manoel dos Santos Francisco his nickname means 'the Wren' and was given to him because of his two twisted feet, which contributed to his delightful dribbling skills. His only defeat in 60 games with Brazil was in his last match, which came against England at the 1966 World Cup finals.

*Mage is the local electoral district.

— HAVE SKATES (AND STICK) WILL TRAVEL —

Michel Petit and JJ Daigneault are the most well-travelled players in ice hockey history. Both began their careers as defensemen for the Vancouver Canucks and went on to play for nine other NHL franchises. After being traded by the Canucks during the 1987–88 season, Petit moved to the New York Rangers, then the Quebec Nordiques, Toronto Maple Leafs, Calgary Flames, Los Angeles Kings, Tampa Bay Lightning, Edmonton Oilers, Philadelphia Flyers and Phoenix Coyotes. In addition, Petit played 19 games for the Canadian national team and had stints with the AHL's Fredericton Express, Detroit Vipers, Las Vegas Thunder and Chicago Wolves of the IHL and the Frankfurt Lions of the German league.

Daigneault left the Canucks at the end of the 1985–86 season and went on to play for the Philadelphia Flyers,

— HAVE SKATES (AND STICK) WILL TRAVEL (CONT'D) —

Montreal Canadiens, St Louis Blues, Pittsburgh Penguins, Anaheim Mighty Ducks, New York Islanders, Nashville Predators, Phoenix Coyotes and Minnesota Wild in the NHL. He also won international honours with the Canadian national team and had seasons with the Hershey Bears, Sherbrooke Canadiens and Worcester IceCats of the AHL and the Cleveland Lumberjacks of the IHL.

— ITALIAN CARS MONOPOLISE FRENCH GRAND PRIX—

Only three cars entered the 1926 French Grand Prix – and they were all Bugattis from Italy.

— STONE SKIPPING —

According to NASSA (North American Stone Skipping Association), the world record for stone skipping, or 'ducks and drakes' as it is known in Britain, is 38 skips, achieved at the Fischer Store Bridge on the Blanco river in Texas by a skipper known as Jerdone. The world record was first recognised by Guinness in 1973, and has to be verified on video. The official adjudicator is the ISSF (International Stone Skipping Federation). In France skipping is known as 'ricochet', while in Ireland it is called 'skiffing'.

— THE INCREDIBLE ZATOPEKS —

Probably the finest husband and wife combination to grace the world of track and field, the Czechoslovaks Emil Zatopek and Dana Zatopkova (née Ingrova) also shared a date of birth (19 September 1922), although Emil was apparently four hours older. Between them they won 13 major championship gold medals, with their finest moment the 1952 Helskinki Olympics. Emil was known as 'The Locomotive' or the 'Bouncing Czech' and his treble of 5,000m, 10,000m and marathon is unlikely to be repeated. It included the legendary episode in the marathon, at which he was a total novice, when he ran alongside the Briton Jim Peters, who he considered the favourite and asked, 'the pace Jim – is it too fast?' Peters was struggling and could only say, in jest, 'Emil, the pace – it is too slow,' shortly after which exchange Zatopek hared off. At the same Olympics, Dana added a gold in the javelin, at which she also won the European title in 1954 and 1958. Zatopek fell out of favour with the communist authorities for the part he played in the 1968 Prague Spring, when he distributed leaflets among the Soviet tanks, and he ended up working as a petrol station attendant and down a mine. After the Velvet Revolution of the 1990s, he was decorated by the Czech leader Vaclav Havel. He died in 2000.

— STEVE REDGRAVE —

Henley rower Steve Redgrave is the only oarsman to win gold medals at five consecutive Olympics...this is how he did it:

1984	Los Angeles	Coxed fours	With Martin Cross, Richard Budgett, Andrew Holmes, Adrian Ellison
1988	Seoul	Coxless pairs	With Holmes and Patrick Sweeney
1992	Barcelona	Coxless pairs	With Matthew Pinsent
1996	Atlanta	Coxless pairs	With Pinsent
2000	Sydney	Coxless fours	With Pinsent, Tim Foster and James Cracknell

— MICK THE MILLER —

Britain's most celebrated greyhound can be seen in the Walter Rothschild Zoological Museum in Tring, Hertfordshire, where he stands in a glass case, having been stuffed after his death on 5 May 1939. The Miller ran 81 times and was first or second in all but five, earning £10,000 in prize money. At the start of his career he was auctioned by his first owner, an Irish parish priest named Father Brophy, at the White City racing track for what in 1929 was a vast sum: 800 guineas (£840).

Blessed with a heart 1½oz (42.5g) larger than the average greyhound, the Miller was the first greyhound to win the English Derby in successive years (1929 and 1930) and the first greyhound to run a 525yd (480m) course in under 30 seconds. A triple of Derbys eluded him, however, as the race was ruled null and void after his clear victory. His owner and trainer did not wish to risk him in the re-run, but were over-ruled by none other than the Prince of Wales, a passionate Miller fan, only for the 80,000 crowd to see the dog finish fourth.

The Miller also starred in the 1934 British film *Wild Boy*, where he played a greyhound kidnapped by a gang of criminals trying to stop him running the Greyhound Derby. Mick escapes, runs to White City and duly wins. If only real life had mirrored fiction.

— THE ONE-EYED CYCLIST —

French cyclist Honoré Barthélemy must rank as one of the most stoical figures in sports history. The loss of an eye in a crash during the 1920 Tour de France did not deter him – he carried on to finish eighth in that year's race. Afterwards he wore a glass eye, which frequently caused infections in the socket and often fell out, including once at the finish line of a stage.

Another sportsman to triumph over physical handicap was the Austrian tennis player Hans Redl. He lost an arm at the battle of Stalingrad during the Second World War, but carried on playing tennis competitively and reached the last 16 at Wimbledon in 1947.

— CHEESE ROLLS —

Some say it began 400 years ago to mark the start of summer, others claim it is related to a much older pagan rite that sought to ensure a good harvest. Either way, every year on the last Bank Holiday in May, thousands gather at Coopers Hill, near Brockworth, Gloucestershire, England, to watch the annual cheese rolling races. At noon, a local dignitary starts the first of four races by rolling a Double Gloucester cheese, measuring about 1ft (30cm) and weighing nearly 8¾lb (4kg), down the grassy hill and runners race off trying to catch it. The winner – and local people take this contest very seriously – gets to keep the cheese.

— THE HARVARD–YALE BOAT RACE —

The oldest inter-collegiate event in the US in any sport, this was first held in 1852, and is now run over a 4-mile (6.4km) course on the Thames River at New London, Connecticut. That makes the event the longest regularly run rowing race apart from the Oxford–Cambridge boat race in England which is 4¼ miles (6.8km). In the 1920s, the event rivalled the English boat race for public support, with crowds of around 100,000 and special 32-car observation trains tracking the boats on the railroad that parallels the river. Harvard won the 2003 race to go 85–53 clear in the series.

— THE BIRTH OF RUGBY LEAGUE —

Batley, Bradford, Brighouse Rangers, Broughton Rangers, Dewsbury, Halifax, Huddersfield, Hull, Hunslet, Leeds, Leigh, Liversedge, Manningham, Oldham, Rochdale Hornets, St Helens, Tyldesley, Wakefield Trinity, Warrington, Widnes, Wigan.

The above are the founder members of the Northern Union, who met on 29 August 1895 at Huddersfield, Yorkshire, to break away from the Rugby Union. Their gripe was over the ruling body's unwillingness to let them compensate players who had to take time off work. In 1922 they changed their name to the Rugby Football League.

— WORLD CUP MASCOTS —

England 1966
World Cup Willie

Mexico 1970
Juanito

West Germany 1974
Tip Tap

Argentina 1978
Gauchito

Spain 1982
Naranjito

Mexico 1986
Pique

Italy 1990
Ciao

USA 1994
Striker

France 1998
Footix

Korea/Japan 2002

COMMON EVENTS IN THE
— NORTH AMERICAN LUMBERJACK GAMES —

Crosscut Sawing, Log Rolling, Bow Sawing, Hot Saw, Underhand Chop, Standing Block Chop, Springboard Chop, Tree Felling, Axe Throwing, Pole Climbing, Tree Topping and Birling.

Birling, according to the website usaxemen.com, is done on 12ft (3.7m) long, lathe turned, cedar logs with varying diameters that range from 12–15in (30–38cm), and are floating in a pool. Contestants roll progressively smaller (faster) logs until someone falls. Matches are normally decided by the best two out of three falls, except in the semi-finals and finals where they are decided by the best three out of five falls. All contests in all divisions are run on a modified double-elimination basis.

Birling is not to be confused with log rolling, which is a timed event where a team of two lumberjacks roll a log for 40ft (12m), touch two poles, and roll the log back. This tests their ability to 'read' the ground and the progress of the log.

Safety precautions include the following: 'the area behind the target must be kept clear of people in an area of at least 30 feet [9.1m] deep by 20 feet [6m] wide. If at all possible a "backstop" should be used.' Ties for placings in axe-throwing are, apparently, decided by 'sudden death'.

— THE FIRST MOTOR RACE... —

...was organised by the French newspaper *Le Petit Journal* between Paris and the Normandy town of Rouen on 22 July 1894. Fastest of the 21 entries was Count de Dion in a steam car that travelled the 79 miles (127km) at an average speed of 11.6mph (18.7kph). However, the race jury decided that De Dion's machine was not a feasible road vehicle and the first prize was split between the next two cars, a Peugeot and a Panhard. By coincidence, Paris to Rouen had already been the route for the first inter-city bicycle race, held in 1869 and won by the Englishman James Moore.

— A SELECTION OF NON-OLYMPIC GAMES —

- **Aalborg Youth Games**: Open to 12–16 year olds from Aalborg, Denmark, and its twin towns.

- **Afro-Asian Games**: Intended to combine the four best teams in basketball, football, and handball, the four best track athletes and two best boxers in each weight class from Africa and Asia. Never materialised.

- **AGBU Games**: Sponsored by Armenian General Benevolent Union for people of Armenian origin.

- **Ataturk Dam International Sports Festival**: Water sports at the Ataturk Dam, largest of 22 dams built on the Tigris and Euphrates Rivers to supply water for irrigation and hydroelectricity.

- **BIMP-EAGA Friendship Games**: The BIMP-EAGA (Brunei-Indonesia-Malaysia-Philippines – East ASEAN Growth Area) was established in 1994; BIMP-EAGA games were first held in 1996 in the Philippines.

- **Counter Olympics**: Sponsored by the Communist Party of the USA in 1932 in Chicago as a direct protest against that year's official Olympic Games. Had an estimated 200–400 participants but few spectators.

- **Festival of the Empire**: Celebrated the coronation of King George V in 1911; the first gathering of Commonwealth nations in a multisport event. Great Britain, Canada, Australasia and South Africa competed in five athletics events, heavyweight boxing, two swimming races, and middleweight wrestling.

- **Games of the Small Countries of Europe**: Contested by Andorra, Cyprus, Iceland, Liechtenstein, Luxembourg, Malta, Monaco and San Marino.

- **Gorge Games**: Celebrate the environment of the Columbia River in the state of Oregon with climbing, kayaking, kite sports, mountain biking, off-road triathlon, outrigger canoe, 49 sailing, trail running and windsurfing.

- **Muslim Women's Games**: International competition for athletes from the strict Islamic countries, avoids their breaking Islamic law by competing in front of men in

inappropriate attire. The opening ceremonies are open to male spectators, the athletes wearing full traditional Islamic dress. The events however are closed to men in any capacity.

- **Robin Hood Games**: Run by CP-ISRA, the Cerebral Palsy International Sports and Recreation Association in Nottingham, England, for athletes with cerebral palsy. Athletics, lawn bowling, cycling, powerlifting, swimming and table tennis are included.

- **SCFA Summer & winter Spartakiade**: The SCFA (the Sports Committee of Friendly Armies) Spartakiades were organised by the armies of the Warsaw Pact from 1953 to 1989.

- **SELL Games**: Originally the 'Baltic Students Olympics', the SELL (Suomi, Estonia, Latvia and Lithuania) games began in 1923, were held until 1938, then restarted in 1998 after a 60-year break.

- **SkyGames**: Ultra endurance running, cycling and skiing events at high altitude. Disciplines include the vertical kilometre (a running race with 1,000m [3,280ft] elevation gain), the SkyBike (road cycling and running uphill with 1,000m [3,280ft] height gain) and SkySki (run and climb to a summit using skis and crampons. and ski down as fast as possible).

- **Winter X Games**: Snowboarding, Snow Mountain Bike Racing, Ice Climbing, Skiboarding, Snocross and Free Skiing.

- **World Games**: The 'Olympics' for sports not included in the Olympic Games, for example: acrobatics, aerobics, aikido, bodybuilding, boule lyonnaise, bowling, ballroom dancing, field archery, fin swimming, fistball (faustball), floorball, indoor tug-of-war, ju-jitsu, karate, korfball, lifesaving, military pentathlon, parachuting, pesapallo, petanque, powerlifting, roller skating, squash, trampoline, triathlon, tug-of-war, tumbling and water skiing.

- **World Corporate Games**: The most inclusive international games, open to everyone with no qualifying standards, divided into age divisions with disabled competitors

— A SELECTION OF NON-OLYMPIC GAMES (CONT'D) —

welcomed. Competitors must be part of a team; these are divided into eight divisions based on size. The Games have raised hundreds of thousands of dollars for charity.

• **World Nature Games:** Began in 1997, focused on outdoor sports such as ballooning, canoeing, fishing, mountain biking, golf, riding, parachuting, rafting, sailing and triathlon.

— RUGBY FIELD POSITIONS —

15 Full Back

13 Outside Centre   12 Inside Centre

14 Right Wing   11 Left Wing

10 Fly-half (stand-off, outside-half)

9 Scrum-half

7 Openside Flanker   8 No 8   6 Blindside Flanker

5 Second-row/Lock   4 Second-row/Lock

3 Tight-head Prop   2 Hooker   1 Loose-hand Prop

— WORLD CUP CONVOY —

The 1970 Daily Mirror World Cup Rally, also known as the London to Mexico Rally, was planned to arrive in Mexico in time for the start of the football World Cup, which took place there that summer. Ninety-six cars, ranging from a VW Beetle to a Rolls Royce, were waved off by England football manager Sir Alf Ramsey at the

start of the 16,241-mile (26,132km) race on 19 April 1970, at Wembley Stadium, London. Competitors crossed northern Europe to Budapest, Belgrade and Sofia, before heading back on a more southerly tack through Milan, Burgos and Lisbon. Cars were then freighted from the Portuguese capital to Rio de Janeiro, where the South American leg of the rally took in Sao Paulo, Montevideo, Buenos Aires, Santiago, Lima, Bogota, Panama and then through Central America to Mexico City. Stages were exceptionally hard, including some as long as 650 miles (100km), and anyone who made it as far as the Colombian port of Cali was counted as a 'finisher'. Among the more unlikely participants were Prince Michael of Kent, in an Austin Maxi, and footballer Jimmy Greaves who, with co-driver Tony Fall, placed a highly creditable sixth. For the record, the rally was won by Hannu Mikkola and Gunnar Palm in a Ford Escort.

RAIN SUSPENDS PLAY...
— AT THE WORLD SNOOKER CHAMPIONSHIPS –

The quarter-final match between Fred Davis and defending champion Alex Higgins at the 1973 World Snooker Championships had to be halted due to rain. A skylight in the roof of the City Exhibition Hall, Manchester, sprung a leak, sending water dripping on to the match table. Play was suspended until the roof was repaired. The delay perhaps put both men off their stride as the title was eventually won by Ray Reardon, who beat Eddie Charlton 31–30 in the final.

A similar incident held up play at the 1999 championships at the Crucible Theatre, Sheffield. Water that had collected on an overhead TV gantry dripped on to the match table during the semi-final between John Higgins and Mark Williams, and play was stopped. Williams went on to win the contest, but lost out in the final to Stephen Hendry.

— THE FIRST SOCCER WORLD CUP FINAL —

In the first World Cup final in 1930 both the Argentina and Uruguay teams insisted the match be played with their ball. The referee ruled that the Argentine ball would be used in the first half and the Uruguayan in the second. Argentina led 2–1 at half time, but Uruguay scored three times in the second half to clinch a 4–2 win.

— ADIDAS – WHAT'S IN A NAME? —

Adidas, one of the world's largest sports shoe and clothing companies, has a name derived from a contraction of its founder's name. Adolf Dassler invented spiked running shoes in the early 1920s and went into business with his brother Rudy to sell them. The company flourished, but in 1949 the two went their separate ways. Adolf, known as Adi, paired his nickname with the first three letters of his surname and set up Adidas in August that year. Rudy set up a rival sports shoe company, Puma, that soon also became world famous.

— THE BAREFOOT OLYMPIAN —

Abebe Bikila of Ethiopia was the first black African to win the marathon at the Olympics. One remarkable aspect of his victory at the 1960 Games in Rome was that he ran barefoot. Bikila underwent an appendectomy just 40 days before the Tokyo marathon four years later, prompting many experts to write off his chances of defending his title, but the athlete confounded expectations by setting a new world record time of 2 hours 12 minutes 11.2 seconds to take gold. A note of farce was added to the occasion when the band at the medal ceremony launched into the Japanese national anthem as he mounted the podium because they did not have the music for the Ethiopian one. A bone fracture forced Bikila, by then 36, to retire from the marathon in Mexico City at the 1968 Games. Sadly, the following year, he was paralysed when he crashed a Volkswagen given to him as a present by the Ethiopian government following his second Olympic victory. Bikila died of a brain haemorrhage on 25 October 1973.

— OJ'S RECORD —

OJ Simpson may be better known now for all the wrong reasons, but let's not forget he first found fame as a great American footballer. Playing for the Buffalo Bills, in 1973 he became the first man in the NFL to rush for more than 2,000 yards in a season. It took a decade for his benchmark figure of 2003 yards to be broken – when the LA Rams's Eric Dickerson rushed for 2,105 yards in 1983, setting a new record that remains unbroken.

— TOTTENHAM ODD SHIRTS —

When Tottenham Hotspur played Coventry City in the 1987 FA Cup final, half the Spurs players wore shirts that did not display their sponsor's 'Holsten' logo. Spurs lost 3–2, with Skipper Gary Mabbutt scoring a decisive own goal in extra time. Mabbutt's shirt, much to the relief of Holsten no doubt, was one of the shirts free from advertising.

— ATHLETES AND STALKERS —

While not attracting as many deranged fans as actors or pop stars, athletes are not immune to the unwanted attentions of obsessive individuals.

• In June 1992, Harry Veltman III was detained in a California mental hospital for three years for sending offensive letters and nude photographs of himself to Olympic gold-medallist skater Katarina Witt.

• In Britain, Gillian Vincent was jailed for a week in 1992 for sending pornography through the post and making obscene phone calls to snooker player Stephen Hendry. Two years later she was again found guilty of harassing Hendry.

• Tennis player Monica Seles was stabbed in the back on court in April 1993 while playing Steffi Graf in a tournament in Hamburg, Germany. Her attacker, Guenter Parche, told police 'Seles had no right to play the world's top player. That was Steffi's place. I love her.'

— ATHLETES AND STALKERS (CONT'D) —

- Kurt Zum Felde was arrested twice for breaking into the home of Steffi Graf and was escorted from the grounds after shouting abuse at her while she was playing on Centre Court at Wimbledon in June 1993. The same year another stalker Michael Salata was convicted of sending death threats to Graf. In 1994 he was arrested again outside her home in Palm Beach, Florida. It was reported the following year that Graf was 'turned into a bundle of nerves' by an obsessed female fan who sat outside her New York apartment.

- Theo Dunkelberg was also escorted from the grounds at the 1993 Wimbledon tournament following a complaint by 18-year-old tennis player Anke Huber. Dunkelberg had been stalking her and sending her gifts for two years and was facing charges for fondling her bottom.

- In December 1993 Robert Wall from Cramlington, Northumberland was jailed for five years for his continual harassment of British Olympic gymnast Lisa Grayson.

- Skaters Jayne Torvill and Christopher Dean obtained a court order against Vanessa-Louise Hardman, who had been following them for ten years. Hardman was ordered not to start a fan club and to stop sending teddy bears to Jayne.
- Henry Lee, a Korean-born surgeon in his 60s, followed golfer Laura Davies around America throughout the early 1990s. Lee proposed several times and wrote to her on a monthly basis.

- In May 1996 Russell Bennett was arrested on the roof of British boxer Chris Eubank's home in Hove, East Sussex, while dressed in boxer shorts and boots.

- Ice skaters Roslyn Sumner and Katarina Witt had a restraining order placed on Jerome Richard Petersen in early 1998. The judge ordered that Petersen was not to go within 100ft of either skater.

- Chinyelu Obue was issued with a caution by police after breaking into footballer David Beckham's Cheshire home in February 2000. Obue was then arrested following a second break-in in July 2001, when it emerged that she had been sending letters and underwear to the footballer

for three years. The following March, she was detained indefinitely under the Mental Health Act after taking a taxi 230 miles from her home in Edinburgh to the Beckhams' home and stealing mail. When arrested she was found to be carrying a knife.

• Tennis player Anna Kournikova received a death threat in July 2000 thought to have been sent by an obsessed fan of Elizabeth Hurley. Kournikova had earlier been widely quoted as saying of the actress: 'She is so ugly'.

— TROTSKY, LENIN AND A ROUND OF GOLF —

In the PG Wodehouse story, The Clicking of Cuthbert, one of the fictional characters, a Russian novelist called Vladimir Brusiloff, describes playing a round of golf with a partner against Trotsky and Lenin. In the game, Trotsky is put off a 2in putt by someone in the crowd attempting to assassinate Lenin who, somewhat shaken himself, misses his next shot. As a result, Brusiloff recounts, 'We win the hole and match and I clean 396,000 roubles, or 15 shillings in your money.'

— THE OXFORD V CAMBRIDGE BOAT RACE —

The first race was held in 1829 at Henley on Thames, and the first one on the current course took place in 1845. The course is 4 miles 374 yards (6.75km) upriver from near Putney Bridge, London, to the finish at Mortlake near Chiswick Bridge. The Light Blues of Cambridge have won the race 77 times; the Dark Blues of Oxford 71. The 1877 race is the only one to have officially ended in a dead heat.

• Apart from the dead heat of 1877, the 2003 race was the closest one ever. Oxford won by just 1ft (0.3m).

• The biggest winning margin came in the 1900 race, which Cambridge won by 20 lengths.

• The Cambridge crew of 1998 hold the course record of 16 minutes 19 seconds.

— THE OXFORD V CAMBRIDGE BOAT RACE (CONT'D) —

- Cambridge have sunk twice, in 1859 and 1978, and Oxford once, in 1925. Both boats sank in 1912 and the race was held again the following day when Oxford won. In 1951, Oxford sank and the race was rescheduled for two days later when Cambridge won.

- In 1981 Sue Brown became the first woman to participate in the Boat Race. She was cox for the victorious Oxford crew in 1981.

- Oarsmen take approximately 600 strokes to complete the course.

- Cambridge hold the record for the longest winning streak in the race's history – 13 successive victories from 1924 to 1936.

- Famous crew members include photographer Lord Snowdon (Cambridge, 1950) and actor Hugh Laurie (Cambridge, 1980) – Snowdon's crew won; Laurie's didn't.

- Olympic winners are well represented, including three-time gold medallist Matthew Pinsent (Oxford, 1990, 1991 and 1993), 1992 gold medallist Jonny Searle (Oxford, 1988–90) and 2000 gold medallists Tim Foster (Oxford, 1997), Luka Grubor (Oxford, 1997), Kieran West (Cambridge, 1999 and 2001) and Andrew Lindsay (Oxford, 1997–99).

— THOU SHALT NOT MISS THE FOOTBALL —

During the 2002 World Cup, football-loving worshippers at St Luke's church in Eccleshill, Bradford, found the vicar, Revd John Hartley, more than willing to accommodate them. He moved a 10:30am service to 3pm, to allow fans to watch England play Sweden that morning, and invited them to wear their football strips to the afternoon service. This included a hymn Hartley had written to the tune of television's popular Match Of The Day theme music and a sermon that delivered the message, 'Make Jesus the centre-forward of your life.'

— UNUSUAL US COLLEGE SPORTS TEAM NICKNAMES —

The likes of Notre Dame's Fighting Irish and the University of Alabama's Crimson Tide may be famous, and there are lots of campus Cougars, Eagles and Lions. But plenty of sports squads at US colleges have nicknames that rank as downright bizarre!

College	Location	Nickname
University of California – Irvine	Irvine, California	Anteaters
University of Delaware	Newark, Delaware	Blue Hens
Purdue University	West Lafayette, Indiana	Boilermakers
Campbell University	Buies Creek, North Carolina	Camels
Bloomfield College	Bloomfield, New Jersey	Deacons
University of Oregon	Eugene, Oregon	Ducks
Hampshire College	Amherst, Massachusetts	Frogs
University of Minnesota	Minneapolis, Minnesota	Golden Gophers
Texas Christian University	Fort Worth, Texas	Horned Frogs
Oregon Institute of Technology	Klamath Falls, Oregon	Hustlin' Owls
Columbia College	Columbia, South Carolina	Koalas
Southwestern College	Winfield, Kansas	Moundbuilders
Whittier College	Whittier, California	Poets
Niagara University	Niagara University, New York	Purple Eagles
University of Hawaii	Honolulu, Hawaii	Rainbows
University of Richmond	Richmond, Virginia	Spiders
Trinity Christian College	Palos Heights, Illinois	Trolls
University of Idaho	Moscow, Idaho	Vandals
New York University	New York, New York	Violets
University of Akron	Akron, Ohio	Zips

— ORIGINS OF TABLE TENNIS —

Table tennis was invented in the 1880s
by English engineer James Gibb, using
prototype balls made from champagne
corks and bats fashioned out of cigar-box
lids. When the game was first introduced
commercially, celluloid balls replaced
the corks. First marketed under the
name Gossima, the game met with
limited success but that changed when
the manufacturer renamed it Ping Pong
in 1901.

— CRICKETING FOOTBALLERS —

Ten professional soccer players who also played first-class cricket:
Ian Botham (Scunthorpe and Somerset)
Brian Close (Bradford City and Yorkshire)
Denis Compton (Arsenal and Middlesex)
Les Compton (Arsenal and Middlesex)
Bill Edrich (Tottenham and Middlesex)
Geoff Hurst (West Ham and Essex)
Arthur Milton (Arsenal and Gloucestershire)
Phil Neale (Liverpool and Worcestershire)
Jim Standen (West Ham and Worcestershire)
Ken Taylor (Huddersfield Town and Yorkshire)

— DAVIS SNOOKERED BY DOGGED TAYLOR —

In the mid-1980s snooker was among the most popular
spectator sports in Britain, with millions of fans tuning in
to watch major tournaments live on TV. Master cue-man
Steve Davis was the era's greatest player and for a time
seemed unbeatable. Davis, who had a reputation for
playing dull but extremely effective snooker, was already
a three times World Champion when he progressed to yet
another final at the Crucible Theatre Sheffield in 1985.
His opponent was to be Dennis Taylor; a decent enough
player but no match for Davis...or so it seemed.

With painful predictability, Davis took the first eight frames, displaying typically ruthless assurance. It was beginning to look like a whitewash and though Taylor smiled on ruefully from his chair, there appeared to be no way back for the likeable Ulsterman. Eight-nil down in a 'best of 35 frames' match, was a fairly desperate position.

Taylor won the 9th frame but lost the 10th. However, after winning a closely fought 11th frame he visibly grew in confidence. The next five frames went the way of the underdog and, at the close of the first day's play, Davis led 9–7. It was nip and tuck for the remainder of the match, although Davis retained a slight advantage throughout. Going into the final session, Taylor trailed 13–11 but an audience of more than 18 million people tuned in; most in the hope of seeing a great comeback completed. They were not disappointed.

At 15–15 the tension became unbearable. Davis drew ahead again, winning two frames to move within touching distance of victory, but even he was beginning to show rare signs of nerves and missed several clear chances to end the game in the 33rd frame. The dogged Taylor was not going to relent, and he took the game into the final frame at 17–17. It was a remarkable comeback but his efforts looked to have been in vain as Davis potted his way to seemingly inevitable victory. He had only to pot the brown to take a 22-point lead with only 18 points left on the table. He missed.

Taylor had a reprieve; he potted brown, blue and pink. It was all down to the black. He tried an ambitious double but was foiled by the jaws of the pocket. An exchange of safety shots followed until Davis made an error and left his opponent with a straightforward shot for victory. It was a shot Taylor would expect to make without any difficulty. But he missed. Taylor slumped to his chair as Davis stepped up to take on a more difficult but eminently potable chance. He missed, too; the crowd gasped and simultaneously chuckled in disbelief. The balls were lined up before the pocket, Taylor took aim and made no mistake. The new champion sunk to his knees and gave thanks for the most amazing comeback in snooker history.

— SKATING JUMPS —

The Salchow

The Axel

The Lutz

— ORIGINS OF SYNCHRONISED SWIMMING —

Although grace underwater was recognised in ancient times, the roots of synchronised swimming can be found in the late 19th-century British fad for 'ornamental' swimming and stunts. Katherine Curtis, a swimming instructor at the University of Chicago, extended the concept in the 1920s by encouraging her classes to combine tricks, strokes and floats in time to music. Her students performed as the Kay Curtis Modern Mermaids to large crowds at the 1933–34 Chicago Fair, where the term synchronised swimming was first coined. In the late 1930s, an intercollegiate competition was proposed, but war delayed the first such national championship until 1946.

— THEY THINK IT'S ALL OVER... —

The USA had never lost a game in Olympic basketball history – until 11 September 1972: the USA v USSR final at the Munich Games that ended with one of the most controversial upsets in sports history. With five minutes to play, the USSR were leading 44–36 when the Americans started to rally. The USA had closed the gap to a single point with just the final few seconds remaining when Doug Collins of Illinois State University was intentionally fouled by Sako Sakandelidze. Officials stopped the clock with three seconds left. Collins made both his free throws, putting the USA ahead by 50–49. The USSR in-bounded the ball and the US team and fans began to celebrate.

No one's quite sure what happened next even though the game was televised around the world. Some say Soviet coach Vladimir Kondrashkin had signalled a timeout but was noticed by only a few officials. Others say either the timeout horn or a klaxon sounded from within the crowd was mistaken for the final horn. Others say head referee Renato Righetto of Brazil stopped the game with a second still on the clock because he had noticed a disturbance at the scorer's table. The decision was made to set the clock back to three seconds and resume play. Another desperation play by the USSR saw the ball thrown the length of the court but falling short of the USA's hoop as the horn sounded for a second time. The Americans resumed their celebrations. But then it was announced that the timekeeping mechanism had malfunctioned. The clock was again reset with three seconds remaining. This time, Ivan Yedeshko threw the ball up court to Alexander Belov, who muscled his way past two US defenders, Jim Forbes and Kevin Joyce, to score. The USSR had won 51–50. The Americans protested furiously, but the appeals jury, which comprised representatives from Hungary, Poland, Cuba, Italy and Puerto Rico, ruled by 3–2 that the final result should stand. The aggrieved American team and coaches refused to attend the awards ceremony or to accept the silver medals, which remain uncollected in a vault in Switzerland.

— FIVE PENALTIES IN HALF AN HOUR —

When Crystal Palace took on Brighton in a Second Division soccer game in March 1989, referee Kelvin Morton made history by awarding five penalties in the space of just 27 minutes. The penalties ran as follows:

Palace are 1–0 up, Brighton are down to ten men and Mark Bright scores to make it 2–0.

Minutes later Palace win another spot-kick. But this time Bright sees his effort saved by keeper John Keeley.

Palace win a third penalty in five minutes. Bright passes responsibility to Ian Wright, who misses.

After a ten-minute period either side of half time without incident, Morton breaks the monotony by awarding another...penalty. This time he gives it to Brighton, who score courtesy of Alan Curbishley. The score is now 2–1 to Palace.

The fifth and final penalty goes to Palace, who miss again, this time through John Pemberton.

The game ended 2–1 to Crystal Palace.

— BARE-KNUCKLE MARATHON —

The longest fight in bare-knuckle boxing history is reputed to be a bout between Jas Kelly and Jonathan Smith, which took place in Melbourne, Australia, in 1893. The fisticuffs lasted for 375 minutes – that's equivalent to 125 rounds.

— CB FRY —

Few athletes can rival the all-round sporting ability of the great CB Fry. The legendary Victorian was an England fast bowler and batsman, held the world long-jump record, played soccer for England (also appearing in an FA Cup final) and was an excellent rugby player. Not bad for a man with only one lung!

— USA SINK ENGLAND —

England, along with hosts Brazil, were favourites for the 1950 World Cup finals. The USA, who had no professional league to draw upon and whose star player was a Scotsman who had been released by Third Division Wrexham, were most certainly not among the pre-tournament favourites. When the two teams met on a bumpy pitch in Belo Horizonte, England were expected to enjoy something akin to shooting practice. An easy victory was apparently assured. However, things did not run to plan. The Americans had not read the script and scored the game's only goal when Gaetjens headed in their only chance. The English quickly began to complain...the crowd were too close, the pitch was too hard, they were still tired from a long season. But the excuses could not disguise the fact that they had lost in humiliating fashion to a team of part-timers from a country that was largely disinterested in soccer.

— INDEX —

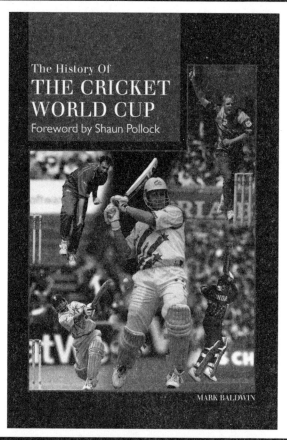

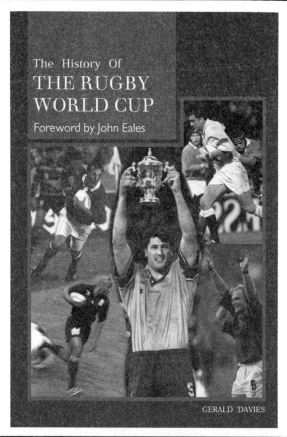